Norwegian Fjords Cruise

Travel Guide 2025

A Comprehensive Companion to Exploring Scenic Routes, Hidden Treasures, and Unforgettable Experiences Across Norway's Majestic Coastline.

Rowan M. Sterling.

COPYRIGHT

All rights reserved. No part of this publication may be reproduced, distributed, or transmitted in any form or by any means, including photocopying, recording, or other electronic or mechanical methods, without the prior written permission of the publisher, except in the case of brief quotations embodied in critical reviews and certain other non-commercial uses permitted by copyright law.

Copyright © 2025 by Rowan M. Sterling.

NORWEGIAN FJORDS CRUISE

HOW TO SCAN QR-CODE

Open the Camera App:
Start by unlocking your smartphone or tablet. Open the default camera app on your device. This step is crucial as some devices can scan QR codes directly from the camera app.

Position the QR Code:
Hold your device steady and point the camera towards the QR code you want to scan. Ensure that the QR code is well-lit and within the frame of your camera.

Focus and Scan:
Your device's camera will automatically focus on the QR code. Wait for a moment until your device recognizes the QR code. You might see a notification or a pop-up indicating that the QR code has been detected.

Tap on the Notification:
If your device doesn't automatically recognize the QR code, you might need to tap on the screen where the QR code is visible. This action helps your device focus and scan the code.

Follow the Link or Action:
Once the QR code is successfully scanned, your device will typically display the associated information. This could be a website URL, contact information, app download link, or any other action associated with the QR code. Follow the displayed instructions or access the linked content.

By following these steps, you'll be able to easily scan QR codes using your smartphone or tablet camera. If your device doesn't support scanning QR codes directly from the camera app, you can download a QR code scanner app from your device's app store.

3 | Norwegian Fjords Cruise Travel Guide 2025

4 | Norwegian Fjords Cruise Travel Guide 2025

5 | Norwegian Fjords Cruise Travel Guide 2025

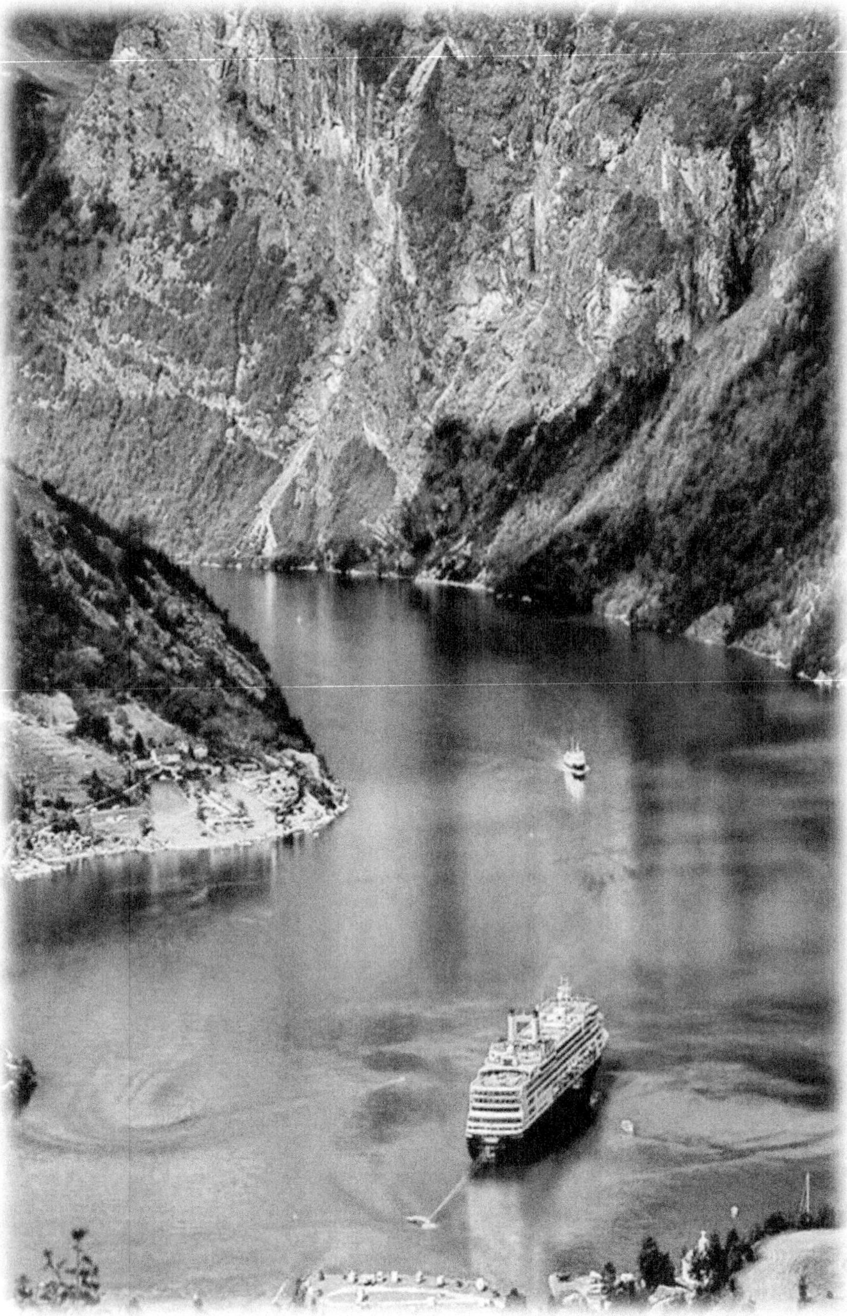

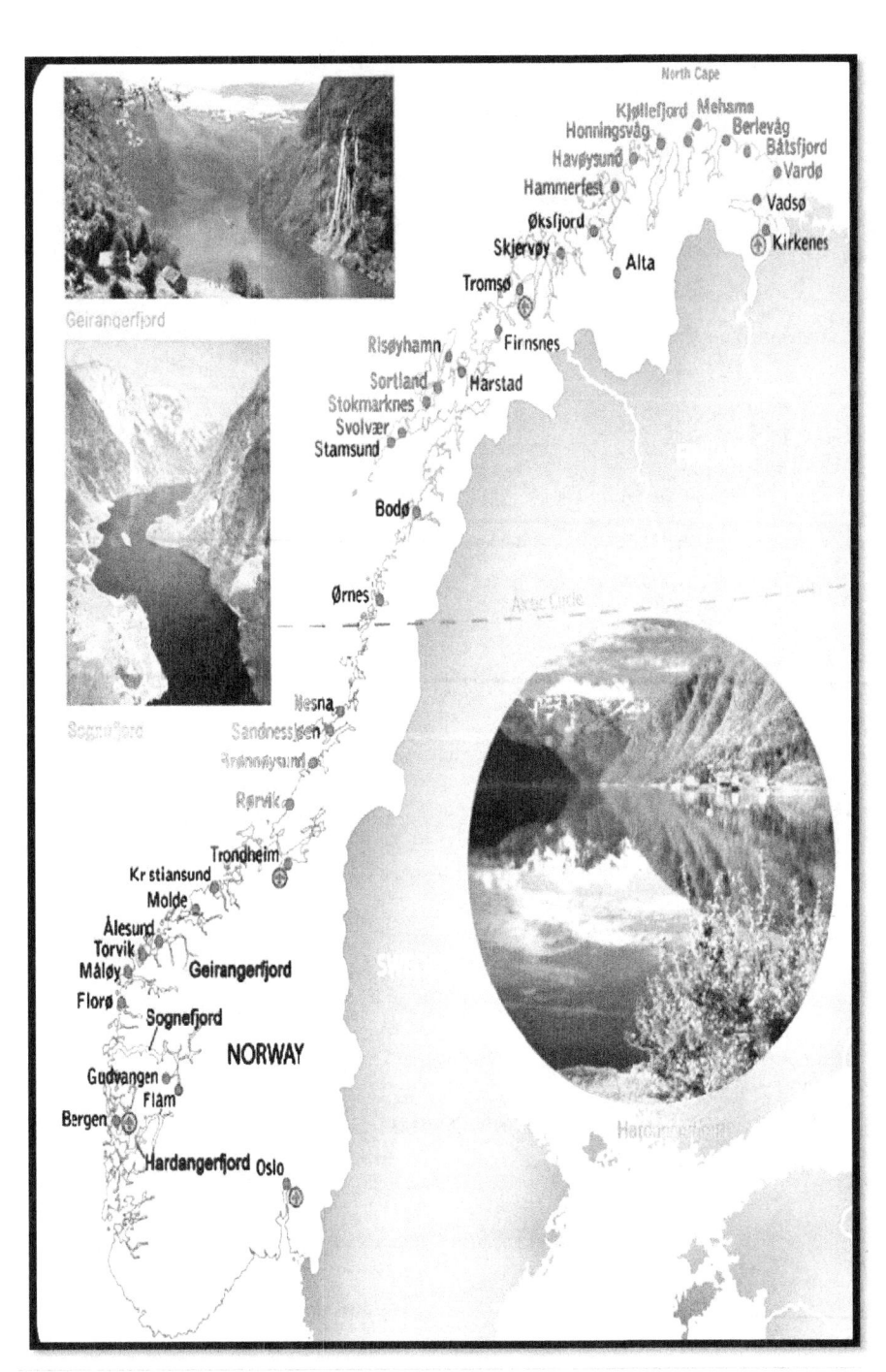

Geirangerfjord

Sognefjord

Norwegian Fjords Cruise Travel Guide 2025

TABLE OF CONTENTS

INTRODUCTION 15

    OVERVIEW OF THE NORWEGIAN FJORDS 15
    WHY A CRUISE IS THE BEST WAY TO EXPERIENCE THE FJORDS 17
    WHY VISIT THE NORWEGIAN FJORDS IN 2025? 19
    HOW TO USE THIS GUIDE 21

CHAPTER 1 23

    CHOOSING THE RIGHT CRUISE LINE FOR YOUR NORWEGIAN FJORDS ADVENTURE ... 23
    CHOOSING THE RIGHT CRUISE LINE 24
    BEST TIME TO VISIT THE NORWEGIAN FJORDS 26
    DIFFERENT TYPES OF CRUISES (LUXURY, EXPEDITION, FAMILY, ETC.) 28
    KEY PORTS OF CALL AND THEIR ATTRACTIONS 31
    CRUISE DURATION AND ITINERARY OPTIONS 41
    WHAT'S INCLUDED IN A NORWEGIAN FJORDS CRUISE 43

CHAPTER 2 46

    BOOKING YOUR CRUISE: TIPS AND BEST PRACTICES 47
    BOOKING YOUR CRUISE 48
    PACKING FOR A FJORD CRUISE 51
    WHAT TO EXPECT ONBOARD: CRUISE SHIP AMENITIES AND SERVICES 54
    HEALTH AND SAFETY CONSIDERATIONS 57
    TRAVEL INSURANCE: IS IT WORTH IT? 59
    CURRENCY, ELECTRICAL OUTLETS, AND LOCAL CUSTOMS 61

CHAPTER 3 65

    ARRIVAL AT THE PORT: WHAT TO DO BEFORE BOARDING 65
    ARRIVAL AT THE PORT 66
    FIRST IMPRESSIONS: EXPLORING THE CRUISE SHIP 69

Navigating the Ship: Deck Plans and Key Areas 72

Onboard Etiquette and Dress Code 74

Activities and Entertainment on the Ship 79

CHAPTER 4 85

Exploring Norway's Iconic Fjords and Coastal Cities.. 85

Bergen: The Gateway to the Fjords 86

Visiting Mount Fløyen and the Fløibanen Funicular 89

Excursions Around Bergen 93

Geirangerfjord: The Jewel of the Fjords 95

Hiking and Waterfalls 98

Alesund: Art Nouveau and Panoramic Views 103

The Aksla Viewpoint 106

Tromsø: Gateway to the Arctic 110

Arctic Wildlife and Activities 113

Flåm: The Heart of the Fjords 118

Outdoor Activities in Flåm 123

Stavanger: Norway's Coastal Gem 127

Fjord Adventures & Outdoor Activities in Stavanger 131

CHAPTER 5 139

Adventures in the Norwegian Fjords: Outdoor Activities and Cultural Experiences 139

Hiking and Nature Walks 140

Cycling Through the Fjords 143

Kayaking and RIB Boat Adventures 146

Wildlife Watching: From Whales to Reindeer 149

Exploring Norwegian Culture: Museums, Food, and Local Life 152

Excursions for Adventure Seekers: Glacier Tours, Dog Sledding, and More 156

CHAPTER 6 161

Norwegian Cuisine: What to Expect 161

    Dining Options Onboard: From Buffets to Fine Dining 165

    Drinks and Norwegian Spirits.. 170

    Vegan and Dietary Restrictions: What You Need to Know 173

CHAPTER 7 177

    Norwegian Culture and Traditions 177

    The Sami People and Their Heritage 179

    The Role of the Vikings in Norwegian History 181

CHAPTER 8 185

    Modern Norway: Embracing Sustainability, Innovation, and Language 185

    Sustainability, Design, and Innovation.. 186

    Language Tips: Basic Norwegian Phrases to Know 191

CHAPTER 9 197

    What to Buy: Traditional Handicrafts, Food, and More 197

    Best Shopping Districts and Souvenir Shops 201

    Local Markets and Artisans.. 207

CHAPTER 10 213

    Weather in the Fjords: What to Expect Throughout the Year 213

    Packing for All Seasons: Layering and Waterproof Gear 217

CHAPTER 11 221

    The Midnight Sun: Experiencing the Polar Day.. 221

    Northern Lights: When and Where to See Them 224

CHAPTER 12 231

    Staying Healthy Onboard: Facilities and Services 231

    Medical Emergencies and Cruise Ship Protocols.. 234

    Avoiding Seasickness and Travel Illnesses 236

CHAPTER 13 239

TRAVEL SAFETY: NORWEGIAN LAWS AND CUSTOMS 239

STAYING SAFE WHILE EXPLORING THE SHORE 243

CHAPTER 14 247

RESPONSIBLE TOURISM: PRESERVING THE FJORDS 247

WILDLIFE PROTECTION AND ECO-FRIENDLY ACTIVITIES 250

CHAPTER 15 255

THE ENVIRONMENTAL IMPACT OF THE CRUISE INDUSTRY & SUSTAINABLE TRAVEL IN NORWAY 255

THE CRUISE INDUSTRY'S IMPACT ON THE ENVIRONMENT 256

HOW TO TRAVEL SUSTAINABLY IN NORWAY 259

CHAPTER 16 263

MAXIMIZING YOUR CRUISE EXPERIENCE: MONEY-SAVING TIPS, AND STAYING CONNECTED 263

MONEY-SAVING TIPS: DEALS AND OFFERS 264

GETTING THE BEST PHOTOS OF THE FJORDS 266

HOW TO MAKE THE MOST OF YOUR SHORE TIME 269

STAYING CONNECTED: WI-FI, PHONE, AND ROAMING INFORMATION 273

CHAPTER 17 277

SAMPLE ITINERARIES FOR EVERY TRAVELER: A COMPREHENSIVE GUIDE TO EXPLORING THE NORWEGIAN
FJORDS 277

ONE-DAY ITINERARY: A COMPLETE NORWEGIAN FJORDS EXPERIENCE 278

THREE-DAY ITINERARY: EXPLORING THE WONDERS OF NORWAY'S FJORDS 280

SEVEN-DAY, NORWEGIAN FJORDS ITINERARY: A COMPLETE WEEK OF ADVENTURE AND CULTURE 282

THREE-DAY OUTDOOR ADVENTURE AND NATURE LOVERS' ITINERARY IN THE NORWEGIAN FJORDS .. 284

THREE-DAY ROMANTIC GETAWAY IN THE NORWEGIAN FJORDS 285

THREE-DAY FAMILY FUN ITINERARY IN THE NORWEGIAN FJORDS 286

CHAPTER 18 287

ESSENTIAL APPS, RESOURCES, AND CONTACTS FOR YOUR NORWEGIAN FJORDS ADVENTURE 287

ESSENTIAL TRAVEL APPS FOR THE NORWEGIAN FJORDS 288

OFFICIAL TOURIST INFORMATION AND VISITOR CONTACTS FOR THE NORWEGIAN FJORDS 293

LOCAL GUIDES AND OPERATORS FOR YOUR NORWEGIAN FJORDS CRUISE TRAVEL 298

USEFUL WEBSITES FOR CRUISE BOOKINGS AND PLANNING 301

CONCLUSION 305

TRAVEL PLANNER... 308

13 | Norwegian Fjords Cruise Travel Guide 2025

14 | Norwegian Fjords Cruise Travel Guide 2025

Introduction

Overview of the Norwegian Fjords

Imagine cruising through the most stunning landscapes you've ever seen—towering cliffs, deep blue waters, and cascading waterfalls. Welcome to the Norwegian Fjords, one of the most spectacular natural wonders on the planet. Nestled along Norway's western coastline, these fjords are not just bodies of water; they are channels of history, culture, and nature that have shaped the people who live here for centuries.

The word *"fjord"* itself is derived from the Old Norse term for a "long, narrow sea inlet between cliffs," and that's exactly what they are. Formed by ancient glaciers that carved deep valleys through the rugged mountains, the fjords are incredibly scenic and offer jaw-dropping views. With over 1,000 fjords in Norway, you'll be spoilt for choice when it comes to exploring these majestic waterways.

The most famous of them all is the **Geirangerfjord**, known for its steep cliffs and waterfalls, like the **Seven Sisters**. The **Sognefjord**, the longest in Norway, stretches for over 200 kilometers, with dramatic mountain peaks that rise sharply from the sea. But there's much more to the fjords than just scenic beauty. These waters have been the lifeblood of Norway, offering a route for trade, migration, and culture for thousands of years.

Why a Cruise is the Best Way to Experience the Fjords

There are many ways to explore the Norwegian Fjords, but none compare to experiencing them by cruise. Why? Because a cruise allows you to see the fjords from the water, where they truly come alive in all their grandeur. Whether you're gliding past lush green hillsides or getting up close to waterfalls that tumble from dramatic cliffs, being on the water offers an unparalleled perspective.

One of the most magical things about a cruise through the fjords is the way the scenery constantly changes. As you move along, you'll encounter new and breathtaking views with every turn. Around each bend, the towering mountains seem to reach for the sky, while picturesque villages dot the landscape below. There's no better way to immerse yourself in the natural beauty of this part of the world.

Aside from the views, cruising through the fjords also offers the opportunity to visit remote and charming towns that you can't easily access by other means. Places like **Flam** and **Bergen** are popular cruise stops, where you'll have a chance to explore the local culture, visit historic sites, and sample traditional

Norwegian cuisine. Plus, many cruises include guided shore excursions to attractions like the **Flåm Railway**, one of the world's steepest railways, or the iconic **Preikestolen** (Pulpit Rock) hike overlooking the Lysefjord.

And then there's the convenience factor. A cruise allows you to visit multiple destinations in one trip, without the hassle of packing and unpacking, or worrying about transportation between cities. Your floating hotel takes you from one breathtaking destination to the next, all while you relax, enjoy the onboard amenities, and let the scenery unfold around you.

Why Visit the Norwegian Fjords in 2025?

The Norwegian Fjords have long been a top destination for travelers seeking natural beauty and a tranquil escape. However, 2025 is shaping up to be an exceptional year to explore these magnificent landscapes, with new developments, enhanced experiences, and exciting events that promise to take your visit to the next level.

In 2025, the Norwegian Fjords will see a renewed focus on sustainable tourism, with more eco-friendly initiatives and infrastructure improvements. New hiking trails are being introduced, especially in areas like the **Lofoten Islands** and **Geirangerfjord**, allowing visitors to experience the raw beauty of the landscape while minimizing their environmental impact. Many fjord cruises are now incorporating **electric boats** or **liquefied natural gas (LNG) powered ships**, offering a cleaner way to explore these majestic waterways. Norway's push for green tourism is particularly evident in **Norway's Scenic Routes**, where new eco-conscious measures are in place to preserve the pristine nature of the fjords and surrounding areas.

The region is also seeing an **increased investment in nature-based experiences**. For 2025, **new hiking trails** and **scenic**

viewpoints have been established, particularly in the areas surrounding **Geirangerfjord** and **Sognefjord**. These trails offer not only incredible views of the fjords' towering cliffs and cascading waterfalls, but they are also designed to offer an immersive experience in Norway's unique **flora and fauna**. Whether you're an avid hiker or someone who prefers a more leisurely walk, the trails cater to all levels of adventurer.

Norway's fjords are also embracing **new adventure tourism opportunities** in 2025. Whether it's **kayaking through narrow fjords**, **snowshoeing across glacier fields**, or embarking on a **dog sledding adventure** in the Arctic, there's no shortage of ways to get up close and personal with nature. In **Flåm**, the legendary **Flåm Railway** is also expanding its offerings, providing even more routes for travelers to take in the **breathtaking scenery** in style and comfort.

Whether you're seeking adventure, relaxation, or a deeper connection with the environment, the fjords in 2025 promise a journey that will stay with you long after you've left. Norway is waiting, ready to show you the wonders of its fjords—and this time, they're more breathtaking than ever. *Are you ready to experience them?*

How to Use This Guide

This guide is designed to be your trusted companion throughout your journey in the Norwegian Fjords. Whether you're planning your trip from home or already exploring the stunning landscapes, this guide offers practical advice, detailed insights, and personalized itineraries to ensure you make the most of your time in the Norwegian Fjords. It is organized in a way that allows you to easily navigate through the various aspects of your trip, making it simple to find the information that's most relevant to your needs.

Begin by reading the *Introduction* section to get an overview of the fjords and understand why they are one of the most sought-after destinations. It will set the stage for your adventure, introducing the key highlights, the region's rich history, and what makes 2025 a particularly exciting year to visit.

Chapter 1 is the starting point for practicalities. It provides essential information on **choosing the right cruise line** for your trip, when to visit, and the various types of cruises available. You'll learn about the **key ports of call**, cruise durations, and itineraries, helping you plan your time wisely and decide how to get the most out of your trip.

As you flip through the chapters, you'll dive deeper into everything from booking your cruise and packing tips in **Chapter 2**, to exploring the iconic fjords and cities like **Bergen** and **Geiranger** in **Chapter 4**. For nature lovers, **Chapter 5** offers exciting **outdoor activities** like hiking and kayaking.

For those interested in Norwegian culture, **Chapter 7** gives an in-depth look at the country's traditions, cuisine, and crafts. If you're looking for practical advice, **Chapter 9** will guide you on budgeting, safety, and local customs, while **Chapter 10** emphasizes **eco-friendly travel** in Norway.

As you plan your trip, **Chapter 17's Sample Itineraries** offer you tailored suggestions for different trip lengths and traveler types. Whether you're visiting for a short weekend or a week-long adventure, these itineraries ensure that you don't miss out on the best the Norwegian Fjords have to offer.

This guide is designed to be flexible and easy to navigate, allowing you to jump directly to the sections that match your needs. It's here to help you plan and enhance your journey every step of the way. **Enjoy your adventure in the Norwegian Fjords!**

Chapter 1

Choosing the Right Cruise Line for Your Norwegian Fjords Adventure

---

Sailing through the **Norwegian Fjords** is a breathtaking experience, but selecting the right cruise line is essential to ensure the best journey. Whether you're seeking a **luxury escape, a family-friendly adventure, or an expedition-style voyage**, each cruise line offers a unique experience.

This chapter explores **the best cruise lines for different travelers**, from high-end ships with world-class amenities to smaller expedition vessels designed for exploring remote fjords. It also provides insights into **seasonal factors**, helping you determine the **best time to visit** for clear skies, wildlife spotting, and fewer crowds.

Additionally, we'll cover the **key ports of call**, highlighting their must-visit attractions, and break down **itinerary options** to suit different trip lengths. Finally, you'll find details on **what's included in a Norwegian Fjords cruise**, ensuring you know exactly what to expect before setting sail on this unforgettable journey.

Choosing the Right Cruise Line

Planning a cruise to the Norwegian Fjords is exciting, but with so many cruise lines to choose from, it can feel overwhelming. The good news is that each cruise line offers something unique, and finding the right one depends on your preferences and what you want to experience.

Start by considering the kind of atmosphere you want on board. Some cruise lines are known for their luxury, offering fine dining, expansive suites, and top-notch service. If that's what you're looking for, you might want to explore lines like **Regent Seven Seas Cruises** or **Viking Ocean Cruises**. These cruise lines offer all-inclusive packages that include shore excursions, drinks, and even gratuities, so you won't have to worry about extra costs once you're on board.

On the other hand, if you're looking for something a bit more adventurous, an expedition-style cruise could be the way to go. **Hurtigruten** is a leader in this category, providing a more intimate and active experience, including options for hiking and kayaking along the fjords. This is ideal if you want to get up close to nature and have a more hands-on experience during your stops.

For families, there are plenty of cruise lines that cater specifically to young travelers. **Disney Cruise Line** and **Royal Caribbean** are excellent choices for families, offering activities for kids of all ages, from water parks to kids' clubs. These cruises also tend to have family-friendly shore excursions, such as trips to Viking museums or easy hikes with scenic views.

Finally, consider the size of the ship. Larger ships often offer more amenities like pools, spas, and a variety of dining options, while smaller ships can take you to more remote locations, offering a more intimate experience. Smaller ships are also less likely to have the crowds that come with larger ships, which might make your trip feel more personal and less rushed.

When you're choosing a cruise line, make sure to research their itineraries to ensure they visit the fjords you want to see. Many cruise lines offer customizable options, so you can decide whether you want a longer or shorter trip, or if you'd prefer to focus on specific regions of Norway. Don't forget to also read up on their cancellation policies, what's included in the price, and their reputation for service and customer satisfaction.

Best Time to Visit the Norwegian Fjords

Norway's beauty is truly year-round, but when you should visit the fjords depends on what you want to experience.

Summer (June to August) is the most popular time to visit. The weather is milder, with average temperatures ranging from 15°C to 20°C (59°F to 68°F), although it can still feel chilly near the water. Summer also means long days, with the famous **Midnight Sun** in the far north. In the summer months, you'll have more hours of daylight to explore the fjords, making it the best time for outdoor activities like hiking, biking, or just soaking in the views. It's also the best time for families, as the weather is generally more comfortable for kids and excursions are plentiful.

Spring (April to May) and **Autumn (September to October)** are quieter times to visit the fjords. The weather can be unpredictable, with temperatures ranging from 5°C to 15°C (41°F to 59°F), and you might encounter occasional rain or chilly winds. However, these seasons offer fewer tourists, so you'll have a more peaceful and intimate experience. Autumn also brings stunning fall foliage, especially in the areas around **Geirangerfjord** and **Sognefjord**. These months are perfect for travelers looking to avoid the crowds and enjoy the fjords with a bit more solitude.

Winter (November to March) is for the more adventurous. The fjords look entirely different under a blanket of snow, and the chance to see the **Northern Lights** is a huge draw for winter travelers. However, winter is also much colder, with temperatures averaging between -5°C and 5°C (23°F to 41°F). It's the least popular time to cruise the fjords, but for those who enjoy winter sports or the peaceful quiet of winter, it can be a magical time to visit.

Different Types of Cruises (Luxury, Expedition, Family, etc.)

Now that you know when to go, the next step is deciding on the type of cruise that best fits your needs and preferences. Here are the main types of cruises you can choose from:

Luxury Cruises: If you're looking for an all-inclusive experience with high-end service, luxury cruises are the way to go. These cruises cater to those who want the best in comfort, fine dining, and top-tier service. Luxury cruise lines like **Regent Seven Seas** and **Oceania Cruises** offer spacious cabins, many with private balconies and large windows to enjoy the stunning views. These cruises often feature gourmet restaurants, luxurious spa services, and included shore excursions. They tend to attract a more mature crowd, so if you're seeking peace and relaxation in an elegant setting, this is your perfect match.

Expedition Cruises: For those seeking more adventure, expedition cruises are all about getting closer to nature. **Hurtigruten** and **Ponant** are leaders in this category, offering smaller, more intimate ships designed for active travelers. These cruises focus on connecting you to the environment—whether it's through excursions that take you kayaking along the fjords or offering hikes up rugged terrain to reach incredible viewpoints. Expedition cruises also allow you to explore remote areas that larger ships can't reach, and they often have onboard experts who can provide educational talks about the wildlife, history, and ecology of the region.

Family Cruises: Cruises are a fantastic option for families, with many lines offering activities designed for children. **Royal Caribbean** and **Disney Cruise Line** are the go-to for families. Both offer incredible onboard entertainment, including Broadway-style shows, kids' clubs, and water parks. The shore excursions are also family-friendly, often featuring short hikes, cultural activities, and visits to scenic viewpoints that are accessible for all ages. Families can also take advantage of childcare services and family suites that offer more space to spread out and relax after a day of exploration.

Small Ship Cruises: These cruises focus on providing a more intimate experience, with fewer passengers and smaller, more boutique ships. Lines like **Viking Ocean Cruises** and **Windstar Cruises** offer ships that can dock in smaller ports, giving you access to less touristy destinations while still providing comfort and quality. These cruises tend to have a quieter atmosphere, with a focus on relaxation and luxury.

River Cruises: While not strictly focused on the fjords, *river cruises* along Norway's waterways offer a more relaxed way to see the landscapes. These cruises often travel through towns, villages, and scenic riverside views, offering a slower pace that is ideal for travelers who want to take it easy.

Key Ports of Call and Their Attractions

The Norwegian fjords are among the most breathtaking natural wonders in the world, carved over millennia by glaciers and stretching deep into the rugged Scandinavian landscape. These majestic waterways, flanked by towering cliffs, cascading waterfalls, and emerald-green valleys, have long attracted explorers, nature lovers, and cruise passengers eager to experience their serene beauty. A journey through the Norwegian fjords is not just about scenic sailing—it's about discovering picturesque ports, each offering unique experiences, cultural insights, and outdoor adventures.

Here are some of the key ports of call you'll likely visit on your cruise, along with the attractions that make each destination special:

Bergen – The Gateway to the Fjords

Bergen is often the first port of call for many fjord cruises, and it serves as a perfect introduction to Norway's seafaring history and stunning landscapes. Surrounded by seven mountains and facing the North Sea, this historic city is steeped in maritime heritage.

Top Attractions in Bergen:

- **Bryggen Wharf** – This UNESCO-listed **Hanseatic wharf** is a colorful, timber-clad reminder of Bergen's medieval past. Walking through its narrow alleyways offers a glimpse into the city's mercantile history.
- **Fløibanen Funicular** – A must-do in Bergen, this funicular ascends **Mount Fløyen**, offering panoramic views of the city and surrounding fjords.
- **Fish Market (Fisketorget)** – A paradise for seafood lovers, this open-air market offers everything from freshly caught salmon and king crab to traditional Norwegian fish soup.
- **Fantoft Stave Church** – A reconstructed medieval church showcasing Norway's Viking-era wooden architecture.
- **Ulriken Cable Car** – For an even more dramatic view, take the cable car to **Mount Ulriken**, the highest of Bergen's seven mountains. Adventurers can hike or zip-line down for an adrenaline rush.

Bergen also serves as a launching point for excursions into **Hardangerfjord** *and* **Sognefjord**, *two of Norway's most spectacular fjords.*

Geiranger – Norway's Crown Jewel

If there's one fjord that captures the essence of Norway's natural beauty, it's **Geirangerfjord**. This UNESCO World Heritage-listed fjord is known for its sheer cliffs, emerald waters, and dramatic waterfalls.

Top Attractions in Geiranger:

- **Seven Sisters Waterfall** – A series of waterfalls that cascade down the cliffs in delicate, ribbon-like streams. The legend goes that the **Seven Sisters** are pursued by a single waterfall across the fjord, known as **The Suitor**.
- **Ørnesvingen (Eagle's Bend)** – A winding mountain road with sharp hairpin turns, leading to a lookout that offers one of the most spectacular views over the fjord.
- **Flydalsjuvet Viewpoint** – A popular spot for photographers, where visitors can capture the postcard-perfect essence of Geiranger.
- **Kayaking and RIB Boat Tours** – Exploring the fjord by kayak or speedboat offers an intimate experience with its towering cliffs and hidden waterfalls.
- **Dalsnibba Skywalk** – One of Europe's highest fjord viewpoints, offering a jaw-dropping perspective of Geirangerfjord.

Geiranger is small but offers an unforgettable encounter with nature, making it a highlight of any Norwegian fjords' itinerary.

Flåm – The Heart of the Fjords

Flåm is a small yet enchanting village at the end of the **Aurlandsfjord**, a branch of the mighty **Sognefjord**, Norway's longest and deepest fjord. Despite its size, Flåm is one of the most visited cruise ports, primarily due to its railway and breathtaking surroundings.

Top Attractions in Flåm:

- **Flåm Railway (Flåmsbana)** – One of the most scenic train journeys in the world, this railway climbs from sea level to **867 meters in just 20 kilometers**, passing waterfalls, deep valleys, snow-capped mountains, and tunnels.
- **Viking Valley in Gudvangen** – A short trip from Flåm, this reconstructed Viking village offers visitors a chance to experience traditional Norse culture, complete with warriors, blacksmiths, and storytellers.

- **Nærøyfjord** – A UNESCO-listed fjord that is one of the narrowest and most dramatic in Norway. Many visitors take a **fjord safari** or kayak trip here.
- **Stegastein Viewpoint** – A dramatic observation deck extending over the fjord, providing awe-inspiring views of **Aurlandsfjord**.
- **Otternes Farm Village** – A well-preserved farm settlement dating back to the 1700s, offering a glimpse into traditional Norwegian rural life.

Flåm's charm lies in its ability to blend adventure with tranquility. Whether you're cruising through the narrow fjord or cycling down the valley, the experience is nothing short of magical.

Ålesund – The Art Nouveau Gem

Destroyed by fire in 1904, **Ålesund** was rebuilt in the Art Nouveau style, making it one of Norway's most visually striking towns. Surrounded by mountains and fjords, it's a photographer's dream.

Top Attractions in Ålesund:

- **Atlantic Sea Park (Atlanterhavsparken)** – One of Europe's largest saltwater aquariums, offering a chance to see Norwegian marine life up close, including playful seals and formidable cod.

- **Mount Aksla Viewpoint** – A climb up **418 steps** rewards visitors with sweeping views of the town, surrounding fjords, and nearby islands. For those who prefer an easier route, a road and a sightseeing train offer alternative ways to reach the summit.
- **Jugendstilsenteret (Art Nouveau Center)** – An immersive museum showcasing the history of Ålesund's unique architecture and design.
- **Hjørundfjord Excursion** – Less crowded than other fjords, **Hjørundfjord** offers serene beauty and a glimpse of traditional Norwegian farm life.
- **Giske and Godøy Islands** – These nearby islands provide opportunities for scenic drives, historical sites, and pristine beaches.

Ålesund combines urban charm with fjordland beauty, making it a must-visit for architecture enthusiasts and nature lovers alike.

Stavanger – The Gateway to the Pulpit Rock

Stavanger is a dynamic coastal city known for its blend of old-world charm and modern energy. It serves as the starting point for one of Norway's most famous hikes—**Pulpit Rock (Preikestolen)**.

Top Attractions in Stavanger:

- **Pulpit Rock (Preikestolen)** – This iconic cliff towers 604 meters above the Lysefjord and offers one of the most awe-inspiring views in Norway. The hike takes around four hours round trip, but the reward is worth every step.
- **Gamle Stavanger (Old Town)** – Wander through Europe's best-preserved wooden houses, where cobbled streets and white-painted homes transport visitors back in time.
- **Norwegian Petroleum Museum** – A fascinating look into how Norway's oil industry transformed the nation into one of the wealthiest countries in the world. Interactive exhibits make it engaging even for those with little interest in energy production.
- **Sverd i fjell (Swords in Rock)** – A striking monument commemorating the **Battle of Hafrsfjord in 872**, where Norway was unified under one crown.
- **Lysefjord Cruise** – A boat trip along this stunning fjord reveals rugged cliffs, waterfalls, and the dramatic **Kjerag Boulder**.

Stavanger is an excellent mix of outdoor adventure and cultural heritage, making it one of the most engaging ports in the Norwegian fjords.

Tromsø – The Gateway to the Arctic

Though not always included on a fjord cruise, **Tromsø** is a northern highlight, especially in itineraries venturing beyond the fjords towards the **Arctic Circle**.

Top Attractions in Tromsø:

- **Arctic Cathedral** – A striking architectural landmark with a triangular design meant to resemble icebergs and the **Northern Lights**.
- **Fjellheisen Cable Car** – Offers sweeping views over Tromsø and its surrounding mountains and fjords.
- **Northern Lights & Midnight Sun** – Depending on the season, *Tromsø* is either one of the best places to witness the **Aurora Borealis** or experience the eerie beauty of the **Midnight Sun**.
- **Polaria and the Arctic Aquarium** – A museum dedicated to Arctic wildlife, featuring a bearded seal exhibit and interactive displays about the region's harsh but beautiful environment.

- **Dog Sledding & Sami Culture Tours** – Visitors can experience husky sledding and learn about the indigenous Sami people.

Tromsø offers a mix of history, culture, and extreme natural beauty, making it an unforgettable northern stop.

Trondheim – A Historic Viking City

As one of Norway's oldest cities, **Trondheim** is steeped in **Viking history** and home to some of the country's most significant landmarks.

Top Attractions in Trondheim:

- **Nidaros Cathedral** – Norway's most important medieval cathedral, built over the tomb of **Saint Olav**.
- **Old Town Bridge & Bakklandet** – An enchanting wooden bridge and historic district filled with colorful houses and cozy cafés.
- **Ringve Museum** – A fascinating music history museum set in a beautiful mansion.
- **Munkholmen Island** – A former monastery, fortress, and prison, now a scenic escape with a rich history.

Trondheim *is a perfect blend of Viking heritage, medieval architecture, and Scandinavian charm.*

Cruise Duration and Itinerary Options

When it comes to planning your Norwegian Fjords cruise, one of the first decisions you'll need to make is how long you want to be on the water. Cruise durations vary widely, so you can find an option that fits your schedule and your interests.

Short Cruises (4 to 7 days)

If you're short on time but still want to experience the highlights of the Norwegian Fjords, a shorter cruise is a great option. These cruises typically visit key ports like **Bergen**, **Flam,** and **Geiranger**, and often focus on the most scenic parts of the fjords. They're perfect for first-time cruisers or those who have a limited amount of time to spend in Norway.

Medium-Length Cruises (8 to 12 days)

For a more comprehensive exploration of the fjords, opt for a cruise that lasts around 8 to 12 days. These cruises typically visit more ports of call, including smaller, less-visited villages like **Ålesund** or **Tromsø**, in addition to the main fjords. You'll also have more time to enjoy the onboard amenities and excursions, making this a great option for those who want a well-rounded experience.

Long Cruises (13 days or more)

If you're looking for a truly immersive experience, a longer cruise might be the way to go. These cruises often combine the Norwegian Fjords with other Scandinavian destinations, such as **Stockholm**, **Copenhagen**, and **Helsinki**. This allows you to explore the fjords in greater depth, while also discovering more of the Nordic region's stunning landscapes and vibrant cities.

When choosing your cruise, keep in mind that some itineraries may include special events or seasonal highlights, such as the **Northern Lights** in winter or the **Midnight Sun** in the summer months. Be sure to check the details of each itinerary to see what's included and what fits your preferences.

What's Included in a Norwegian Fjords Cruise

One of the most appealing aspects of booking a Norwegian Fjords cruise is that many of the essentials are included in the price. However, the specifics can vary depending on the cruise line, so it's important to understand what you're paying for when you book.

Accommodation:
Your cruise fare will include your cabin or suite for the duration of the trip. The type of cabin you choose will affect the price, with options ranging from interior rooms to more luxurious suites with private balconies. While cabins with windows and balconies offer the best views, they also come at a higher price. Some cruise lines also offer suites with additional perks like butler service and priority boarding.

Meals and Drinks:

Most cruises to the Norwegian Fjords include all meals—breakfast, lunch, and dinner—either in a buffet-style dining area or at specialty restaurants. Onboard dining options range from casual buffets to more formal à la carte options. Some cruise lines offer all-inclusive drink packages, while others may charge for alcoholic beverages separately. Be sure to check what's included with your specific cruise line.

Shore Excursions:

Many cruise lines offer a selection of shore excursions that are included in the price of your cruise. These can range from city tours and museum visits to nature hikes and kayaking trips. Some excursions may come at an additional cost, especially if you're interested in more specialized or guided experiences, so make sure to check what's included before you book.

Entertainment and Activities:

Cruise lines offer a range of onboard entertainment, such as live music, shows, and movies. Some lines also provide enrichment activities, such as lectures or cooking classes, giving you something to do during your free time on the ship. Fitness facilities, pools, and spas are also included in most packages, though there may be additional fees for spa treatments or special classes.

Gratuities and Taxes:

Be aware that while many cruise lines include gratuities in the price, others may charge them separately. Additionally, taxes and port charges are usually added to your final bill, so be sure to budget for these extra costs.

46 | Norwegian Fjords Cruise Travel Guide 2025

Chapter 2

Booking Your Cruise: Tips and Best Practices

Planning a Norwegian Fjords cruise requires more than just choosing a ship—it's about selecting the right itinerary, understanding what's included, and ensuring a seamless experience from start to finish. This chapter provides essential tips for booking your cruise, from choosing the best cruise line based on your travel style to finding the ideal departure dates for stunning fjord scenery.

You'll also learn about key considerations such as cabin selection, onboard dining options, and the benefits of booking excursions in advance. We'll cover strategies for finding the best deals, understanding cancellation policies, and ensuring your cruise package includes everything you need for a stress-free journey.

With practical advice on avoiding hidden costs and making the most of onboard amenities, this chapter ensures that your Norwegian Fjords cruise is not only memorable but also perfectly tailored to your needs.

Booking Your Cruise

Booking a Norwegian Fjords cruise is an exciting first step, but it can also feel like a big task, especially if you've never booked a cruise before. To make sure you're getting the best experience at the best price, here are some tips and best practices to guide you through the process.

Start Early:

The earlier you book your cruise, the better. Norwegian Fjords cruises are especially popular during the summer months, and cabins tend to fill up quickly. Booking well in advance not only gives you a wider choice of cabin types but also helps you lock in the best prices. If you're flexible with your travel dates, you might also find special deals or last-minute offers during the off-season.

Research Different Cruise Lines and Itineraries:

There are many cruise lines to choose from, and each offers a different experience. Whether you're looking for a luxury experience, an adventurous expedition, or a family-friendly cruise, do your research to find a line that fits your style. Also, check the itineraries carefully. While many cruises visit the major fjords like **Geiranger** and **Flam**, some lines might take you to more remote areas that you can't reach on larger ships. Decide whether you'd prefer a shorter cruise or a more extended journey, and consider how much time you want to spend at each port of call.

Check What's Included:

Cruise pricing can be a bit tricky, so make sure you know exactly what's included in the cost of your trip. Some cruise lines include meals, shore excursions, drinks, and gratuities in the price, while others may charge extra for these items. For example, **Viking Ocean Cruises** and **Regent Seven Seas** are known for their all-inclusive pricing, while other lines sometimes charge extra for shore excursions or specialty dining. Make sure you're clear about what's included and what might come with an additional cost so you can budget accordingly.

Consider Upgrading Your Cabin:

While booking an interior cabin is the most budget-friendly option, consider whether upgrading to a cabin with a window or a balcony is worth it for you. With a balcony cabin, you'll be able to enjoy the stunning views of the fjords from the comfort of your room, and it can make your experience feel even more special. If you're unsure about the upgrade, weigh the cost difference against the added experience of having your own private space to watch the scenery unfold.

Look for Deals and Special Offers:

Keep an eye out for special deals, especially during the off-season. Many cruise lines offer promotions like free airfare, discounts on excursions, or onboard spending credits. Signing up for newsletters or following cruise lines on social media can help you stay updated on these deals. Also, consider booking directly through the cruise line's website for potential perks like priority boarding or discounted rates.

Packing for a Fjord Cruise

Packing for a Norwegian Fjords cruise requires a bit of thought, as the weather can vary dramatically throughout the day. You'll want to be prepared for everything from chilly mornings on deck to warmer afternoons on land. Here's a packing guide to make sure you have everything you need:

Clothing:

The key to packing for a fjord cruise is layering. The weather in Norway can change quickly, so you'll want to be able to adjust as needed. For colder mornings or evenings on deck, bring a warm jacket or fleece, along with a scarf and gloves. During the day, when you're on land exploring, you'll most likely experience milder temperatures, so lightweight layers are a good choice. You'll also want a waterproof jacket or a **poncho**, as rain is common, even in summer.

Comfortable Shoes:

You'll be doing a fair amount of walking, whether you're exploring cities, hiking to a scenic viewpoint, or visiting local shops. Make sure to pack comfortable, waterproof shoes. Hiking boots or sturdy sneakers are ideal, especially if you're planning to take part in any outdoor excursions.

Accessories:

A hat and sunglasses are a must, as the sun can be surprisingly strong when you're out on deck. If you're visiting during the summer months, the **Midnight Sun** means you'll have long days with lots of daylight, so a pair of comfortable sunglasses will be handy.

Swimwear and Fitness Gear:

Most cruise ships have pools, hot tubs, or spas, so don't forget your swimwear. It's also recommended that you bring along workout clothes if you plan on using the ship's fitness facilities. A yoga mat or light resistance bands are also good options for staying active while you're on the ship.

Camera or Smartphone:

You'll be surrounded by incredible scenery at every turn, so don't forget your camera or smartphone to capture those unforgettable moments. If you're using your phone, make sure to pack a portable charger so you can keep snapping photos throughout the day.

Personal Items and Toiletries:

While most cruise lines provide basic toiletries, it's a good idea to bring any personal items you need, such as prescription medication, contact lenses, and a toothbrush. If you wear glasses, bring an extra pair in case yours get lost or damaged.

What to Expect Onboard: Cruise Ship Amenities and Services

Once you're aboard your Norwegian Fjords cruise, you'll discover a world of amenities and services designed to make your journey as comfortable and enjoyable as possible. Cruise ships vary, but here's what you can generally expect on most ships:

Dining Options:

Cruise ships offer a range of dining options, from casual buffets to more formal sit-down meals. Most cruise lines include three meals a day in the price of your ticket, with breakfast and lunch often served in a buffet-style restaurant. For dinner, you'll typically have the option of dining in a main dining room, where you can enjoy a multi-course meal, or at specialty restaurants that may come with an additional cost. Some cruises even offer "open seating", meaning you can dine at any time, while others may assign specific dining times to each passenger.

Entertainment:

Cruise ships are known for their onboard entertainment, and your Norwegian Fjords cruise is no different. Expect a variety of activities, such as live music, theatrical performances, and movie nights. Many ships also have lounges or bars where you can relax with a drink and enjoy the company of fellow passengers. If you're interested in educational talks, some cruise lines offer lectures on topics like Viking history, Norwegian culture, and the wildlife of the fjords.

Fitness and Wellness:

Most ships have a fitness center with cardio machines, free weights, and fitness classes, like yoga or spinning. For those looking to relax, the spa will offer treatments like massages, facials, and saunas, helping you unwind after a day of excursions. Be sure to check the ship's schedule for any wellness activities that may be offered.

Excursions and Shore Activities:

During your time in port, there will be plenty of shore excursions to choose from. These can range from scenic bus tours and cultural tours to more adventurous activities like hiking, kayaking, or even dog sledding. Some cruise lines also offer exclusive or private excursions for those looking for a more personalized experience. The good news is that these excursions are often conveniently arranged right from the ship, so you don't have to worry about logistics.

Wi-Fi and Communications:

While you're cruising through the fjords, you may want to stay connected to family or work. Most ships offer Wi-Fi, though the quality can vary, especially in more remote areas. Expect higher fees for internet access, and if you really need to stay connected, it's a good idea to purchase a Wi-Fi package before boarding.

Service and Gratuities:

The service on cruise ships is typically excellent, with crew members ready to assist you at any time. Keep in mind that gratuities may be included in your cruise fare, but if you feel someone went above and beyond, you can always leave an additional tip. Some cruise lines also offer packages for onboard services, like spa treatments, specialty dining, and excursions, so be sure to ask about them when booking.

Health and Safety Considerations

When preparing for your Norwegian Fjords cruise, health and safety should be at the top of your mind. The good news is that Norway is known for its high standards of healthcare and safety, so with just a few simple steps, you can make sure you're well-prepared for the journey.

Medical Care on Board

Cruise ships are equipped with medical facilities and staff, so if you have a minor illness or injury while aboard, you'll have access to medical help. However, it's important to note that medical care on board may come with an additional charge. For this reason, it's a good idea to bring along basic medications you might need, like pain relievers, motion sickness tablets, or any prescriptions you take regularly. Always keep these items in your carry-on bag, as they may be difficult to access once you're settled in your cabin.

Traveling with Medications

If you're bringing prescription medication, make sure to carry enough for the entire duration of the trip, plus a few extra days in case of delays. It's also recommended that you carry a copy of the prescription for any controlled substances, especially if you're flying into Norway. If you're unsure about specific medication rules, you can check with your cruise line or a travel advisor for guidance. You can also find information on Norway's healthcare services on the official Norwegian health website: www.helsenorge.no.

Vaccinations and Health Requirements

While there are no specific vaccination requirements for travelers going to Norway, it's always a good idea to check with your doctor ahead of time, particularly if you're visiting other destinations on your cruise. Also, consider checking travel advisories or any health-related updates for the country. In light of the ongoing global health situation, always ensure you're up-to-date on any required travel restrictions, testing, or health certifications.

Safety in Norway

Norway is one of the safest countries to visit, with low crime rates. However, like anywhere, it's important to remain aware of your surroundings, particularly when you're in more crowded areas, like ports or tourist sites. Also, the weather in the fjords can change rapidly, so always follow safety instructions when embarking on excursions, especially those involving outdoor activities like hiking or kayaking.

Travel Insurance: Is It Worth It?

When you book a cruise, travel insurance might not be the first thing on your mind, but it's definitely something worth considering. While it's not mandatory, it can offer valuable peace of mind during your trip.

What Does Travel Insurance Cover?

Travel insurance generally covers a range of situations, including trip cancellations, medical emergencies, lost luggage, or delays. For a cruise, it's particularly helpful in case of unexpected medical expenses or the need to cancel your trip due to illness or emergencies. For instance, if you fall ill before the cruise or need to cancel due to family emergencies, insurance will help protect your investment. It can also cover you for cancellations due to unexpected weather conditions or delays at sea.

Medical Coverage

While Norway has excellent healthcare, treatment can be expensive for travelers who don't have insurance. If you fall ill or get injured while on your cruise, travel insurance can help cover medical bills. If you're planning on partaking in adventurous excursions, such as hiking, kayaking, or dog sledding, insurance can also cover accidents or emergencies that might occur during those activities. It's important to choose insurance that provides coverage specifically for activities you plan to do while onboard or ashore.

What to Look for in Travel Insurance

Make sure your insurance covers trip interruption or cancellation, lost luggage, emergency medical care, and even medical evacuation if needed. You should also check if the policy covers any activities you plan to do during your cruise, as some activities may require additional coverage. Compare different policies and find one that offers the right balance of cost and coverage for your needs. Popular insurance providers for cruise travelers include **Travel Guard** (www.travelguard.com) and **Allianz Travel** (www.allianztravelinsurance.com).

Currency, Electrical Outlets, and Local Customs

Before setting off on your cruise, it's essential to understand the local currency, electrical outlets, and customs in Norway to ensure a smooth and stress-free experience.

Currency

Norway's official currency is the **Norwegian Krone (NOK)**. You can exchange currency at banks, currency exchange offices, or ATMs found throughout Norwegian ports. However, credit and debit cards are widely accepted, so you don't necessarily need to carry large amounts of cash. Some cruise lines even offer the option to pay for onboard services and shore excursions in NOK or your home currency, depending on your preferences.

It's also worth noting that tipping is not as common in Norway as it is in other countries. Service charges are typically included in bills, so there's no need to tip for services unless you feel the service warrants it. That being said, tipping small amounts in restaurants or for specific services is appreciated but not expected.

Electrical Outlets

Norway uses the **Type C** and **Type F** electrical plugs, which are the same as in most European countries. The standard voltage is **230V**, and the frequency is **50Hz**. If your electronics use a different plug type, you'll need a travel adapter. It's a good idea to bring a universal power adapter that works for all European outlets. Most cruise ships offer standard outlets in cabins for your convenience, but it's always a good idea to double-check with your cruise line ahead of time if you need special adapters for your devices.

Local Customs

Norwegians are known for their hospitality, but they also tend to value personal space and privacy. When you're onshore or in local towns, it's important to be respectful of local customs and traditions. The pace of life in Norway tends to be more relaxed, and people generally keep to themselves in public. A handshake is a common greeting, and it's customary to remove your shoes when entering someone's home.

When it comes to dress, Norway has a casual dress code, especially in smaller towns. However, if you're attending a formal event on your cruise, like a special dinner, it's a good idea to pack something a little more formal. When hiking or exploring, comfortable shoes and weather-appropriate clothing are essential.

If you're planning to interact with locals or visit cultural sites, it's helpful to know a few key phrases in Norwegian, although most Norwegians speak excellent English. Some basic greetings include **"Hei"** (hello) and **"Takk"** (thank you).

64 | Norwegian Fjords Cruise Travel Guide 2025

Chapter 3

Arrival at the Port: What to Do Before Boarding

Arriving at the port is the first step to an unforgettable cruise experience, and knowing what to expect can make the process smooth and stress-free. From check-in procedures to security screenings, this chapter provides essential information on what to do before boarding.

Once at the terminal, passengers must complete check-in, drop off luggage, and go through security. Understanding the required documents, baggage policies, and customs regulations will help avoid delays. This chapter also covers port amenities, including dining, shopping, and waiting lounges, ensuring you make the most of your time before embarkation.

For those arriving early, nearby attractions and last-minute shopping options are highlighted. Whether you're a first-time cruiser or a seasoned traveler, this chapter ensures a hassle-free start to your journey, allowing you to board with confidence and begin your cruise adventure on the right foot.

Arrival at the Port

The anticipation as you arrive at the port is palpable, and now the journey is about to begin. But before you can step onto the ship and sail away into the Norwegian Fjords, there are a few things you need to take care of:

1. Check-in and Security Procedures:

As you approach the cruise terminal, you'll see a bustling atmosphere filled with fellow passengers. The first step is checking in at the terminal. Be sure to have your **boarding pass**, **passport**, and **any required documents** (such as vaccination records or other health-related forms) readily available. These documents will be checked by the cruise staff at the entrance, and they will verify your reservation.

Many cruise lines now offer **online check-in** ahead of time, which saves you time at the terminal. You'll usually be asked to print out a boarding pass or download it to your phone. Some lines also send **boarding instructions via email** ahead of time, which can provide important details like the specific terminal to go to, the best time to arrive, and any documentation you need to bring.

After check-in, you'll go through a **security screening**, which is similar to airport security. You'll need to place your bags on a conveyor belt for scanning and pass through a metal detector. This process is in place to ensure the safety and comfort of all passengers. Afterward, you'll receive your **key card**—this will serve as your cabin key, identification, and payment method for anything purchased onboard.

2. Luggage Drop-Off:

Once you've checked in, it's time to drop off your luggage. Cruise lines typically handle luggage transportation from the terminal to your stateroom. Be sure to have your **luggage tags** properly affixed to your bags before arriving at the port. These tags are usually sent to you before your cruise, and they'll make sure your luggage is delivered directly to your cabin.

Keep in mind that luggage drop-off can take some time, and your bags won't arrive in your room immediately. **Essentials**—such as medications, documents, and anything you'll need during embarkation—should be packed in your carry-on bag. This ensures you'll have easy access to everything you need before your luggage arrives in your stateroom.

3. Boarding the Ship:

Now comes the exciting moment of boarding the ship. Once security is cleared and luggage is dropped off, you'll follow the signs or be directed to a designated **boarding area**. Depending on the cruise line, there might be a **boarding lounge** where you can relax before the boarding process begins. This area will usually offer some light snacks, beverages, and seating.

When your boarding group is called, you'll be escorted onto the ship. The moment you step onto the ship, the adventure truly begins. Your first impression of the ship's interior will likely be a grand lobby, often featuring stunning decor, large chandeliers, and comfortable seating areas. It's an exciting moment—your floating home for the next several days.

First Impressions: Exploring the Cruise Ship

Your first steps onto the ship are nothing short of awe-inspiring. You'll soon realize that the cruise ship is a city on the water, packed with a variety of amenities and spaces designed to make your time onboard as comfortable and enjoyable as possible. Here's what to expect as you explore your new floating home.

1. The Ship's Interior:

Cruise ships are designed to be welcoming, with spacious **public areas**, wide **corridors**, and panoramic **windows** offering breathtaking views of the sea. The moment you step onboard, take in the atmosphere—whether it's a vibrant art-deco style, modern minimalism, or classic elegance. The ship's interior often features beautiful **atriums** or grand foyers where you'll find seating areas, often adorned with lush plants, decorative items, or even artwork created by local artists.

2. Dining and Entertainment Areas:

One of the highlights of any cruise is the onboard dining, and you'll find several options throughout the ship.

- **Main Dining Room**: This is usually the most formal option, offering multiple-course meals in an elegant setting. Most cruise lines will have a **set dining time**, though some offer **open seating**, which gives you flexibility in when you dine.

- **Buffet or Casual Dining**: On the higher decks, you'll find a buffet or casual dining area where you can eat at your leisure, with a variety of international dishes and live cooking stations.

- **Specialty Restaurants**: Cruise ships often feature one or more specialty restaurants. These venues often require reservations and may charge a cover fee. Some popular options include Italian, Japanese, or French cuisine.

As for **entertainment**, most ships feature an **onboard theatre**, where you can enjoy Broadway-style shows, live music performances, comedy acts, and more. If you prefer a quieter experience, there are often **lounges** with live bands or piano music. Many ships also offer **cinema screenings** for movies, as well as **dance floors** for those looking to enjoy the nightlife.

3. Staterooms and Public Areas:

Next, head to your cabin to check out your home away from home. Depending on your booking, you may have an interior room with no windows, an ocean view room, or a suite with a balcony. All rooms are equipped with basic amenities like a

comfortable bed, **storage space**, **bathroom**, and **TV**. You'll also find towels, a hairdryer, and toiletries ready for your use.

In the public areas, the ship often has a variety of spaces to relax. There are typically **lounges**, **bars**, and **coffee shops** for casual hangouts. If you want to stay active, you might find a **fitness center**, **running track**, or **basketball court** on higher decks. There's usually an **outdoor pool** and hot tubs on the upper decks as well.

If you're in the mood for shopping, most ships have **duty-free shops** selling everything from luxury items to local souvenirs. You'll also find smaller **boutiques** selling clothing, accessories, and jewelry.

Navigating the Ship: Deck Plans and Key Areas

As you continue to explore the ship, it's important to get familiar with the layout. Cruise ships can be massive, so knowing where key areas are will help you move around more easily.

1. Finding Your Way Around:

When you board, the first thing you'll receive is usually a **deck plan**, which outlines the layout of all the ship's decks and their facilities. These plans are posted throughout the ship, and you can always ask crew members for directions. Most ships also have a **digital interactive map** available on your key card or a shipboard app that you can use to find specific areas.

Cruise ships are divided into **several decks**, each with its own purpose. **Public decks** (like the pool deck, dining rooms, lounges, and entertainment areas) are usually located on the higher levels, while **staterooms** are on the lower levels.

2. Key Areas to Know:

- **Dining and Entertainment Venues:** These are usually spread out across different decks. The **main dining room** is often located on a lower deck, while **specialty restaurants** and **buffet areas** are on mid-to-upper decks. **Theaters** or **show lounges** are typically on the lower decks, too.

- **Spa, Gym, and Pools:** You'll typically find the **spa** and **fitness center** on higher decks, offering panoramic views as you exercise. Pools are usually located on the top deck, sometimes with hot tubs and a **bar** nearby.

- **Shops and Boutiques:** These are often located on lower decks, near the lobby area, where passengers can explore duty-free shopping or pick up any last-minute essentials.

- **Public Areas: Lounges, bars,** and **game rooms** are usually spread out throughout the ship, offering a variety of activities for relaxation and entertainment.

3. Emergency Procedures:

Safety is a priority on any cruise, and knowing the location of **emergency exits** and **muster stations** (where you'll gather during a safety drill) is essential. Your muster station and evacuation route will be listed on your **key card** or **room door**. There will also be a **muster drill** early in the cruise, where you'll practice what to do in case of an emergency.

Onboard Etiquette and Dress Code

When you step aboard a cruise ship, you're entering a floating world where you'll be spending several days with fellow passengers. To ensure that everyone enjoys their experience and feels comfortable, it's important to be aware of onboard etiquette and dress codes.

1. Onboard Etiquette:

Cruise ships are all about creating a relaxed, friendly environment, but certain manners and behaviors can help everyone feel at ease. Here's what you should keep in mind:

Respecting Personal Space:

While everyone is there to have fun, it's important to remember that personal space matters. Cruise ships can be busy, especially during peak times like meal times or when embarking and disembarking at port stops. Try to avoid crowding hallways or blocking doorways, and be mindful of others when using shared spaces like lounges or elevators.

Polite and Courteous Behavior:

A simple smile and a "hello" can go a long way in creating a welcoming atmosphere. If you're unsure of something, don't hesitate to ask the crew. They are there to help, and they can guide you to your destination or answer any questions you have.

Being Mindful of Noise:

Since cruise ships are large but still confined spaces, it's important to be mindful of noise levels. If you're in public areas like lounges or corridors, keep conversations at a moderate level so that others can relax. This is especially important when others might be trying to sleep or rest in quieter areas of the ship.

Smoking Areas:

Cruise ships typically have designated smoking areas for passengers who smoke. These areas are often on open decks and in specific parts of the ship. Smoking outside these areas is not allowed, so it's important to respect these boundaries to maintain a comfortable environment for everyone.

Gratuities:

Tipping etiquette can vary between cruise lines, but most ships operate on a **mandatory gratuity system**, which is added to your final bill. This is often a daily charge that covers the crew's tips for their service. If you feel that a crew member has gone above and beyond, you can always leave an additional tip for outstanding service. It's always a good idea to check with the cruise line before you board to understand their specific tipping policies.

2. Dress Code:

The dress code on cruise ships can vary, but in general, you can expect a mix of casual and semi-formal attire. Here's a breakdown of what to expect for different occasions:

Casual Daywear:

During the day, the dress code is typically casual. You'll see passengers in comfortable clothing, such as **T-shirts**, **shorts**, **sundresses**, and **comfortable shoes** for excursions and onboard relaxation. For outdoor activities, like lounging by the pool or attending a shore excursion, casual wear is perfectly acceptable. Make sure to bring a **swimwear** if you plan to spend time by the pool or in the hot tub.

Smart Casual:

For dinners in the main dining room or specialty restaurants, most cruise lines encourage a **smart-casual** dress code. This usually means **collared shirts**, **casual dresses**, **blouses**, **slacks**, and **neat shoes**. You can usually skip the formalwear for these meals, but it's always a good idea to check your cruise line's specific guidelines. For men, button-up shirt and nice trousers are generally acceptable. Women can opt for a simple dress, or a blouse with trousers.

Formal Nights:

Many cruise ships hold **formal nights**, typically once or twice during your voyage. These are special occasions when passengers are encouraged to dress up for dinner and events. For men, this usually means wearing a **suit** or **tuxedo**. For women, a **cocktail dress** or **evening gown** is appropriate. On formal nights, the cruise line will often host **gala dinners**, and there are usually **photo opportunities** in front of backdrops or elegant settings.

Poolside Attire:

When relaxing by the pool or enjoying outdoor spaces, swimwear is acceptable, but it's important to remember that you should wear a **cover-up** when going into indoor areas like restaurants, shops, or lounges. Most cruise lines also request that guests do not wear swimwear to meals in the dining rooms.

Footwear:

Comfortable shoes are essential on a cruise, especially if you plan on taking part in shore excursions or spending time walking around the ship. Comfortable sandals, sneakers, and flip-flops are all appropriate for casual wear. For formal events, you'll want to bring a pair of **dress shoes** to match your attire.

Activities and Entertainment on the Ship

Cruise ships offer a wide variety of activities to keep you entertained throughout your voyage. Whether you're seeking relaxation, adventure, or cultural enrichment, there's always something happening onboard.

1. Daily Activities:

Cruise ships are packed with things to do, and there's no shortage of options to fill your day with excitement. Each day, the **daily newsletter** (often delivered to your room or available at guest services) will list all the scheduled activities and events. From morning to evening, here's a sample of what you might find:

Fitness Classes:

Many cruise ships have state-of-the-art **fitness centers** where you can enjoy everything from **yoga** and **pilates** to **spin classes** and **aerobics**. Some ships even offer unique activities like **Zumba** or **boot camp-style classes**. If you're interested in staying active during your trip, check the daily schedule for workout sessions.

Onboard Games and Competitions:

Get your competitive spirit going with **trivia competitions**, **bingo**, or **game shows** that are often held throughout the day. Some ships offer **art auctions**, **cooking classes**, or even **dance lessons**, where you can learn everything from ballroom dancing to line dancing.

Lectures and Enrichment Talks:

Many cruise lines offer **enrichment lectures** during the day, where experts share insights about the destinations you're visiting. For example, you might learn about **Norwegian history**, **wildlife** in the fjords, or **local art** and **culture**. These talks are usually held in a lounge or theater and are perfect for anyone who wants to dive deeper into the area's heritage and history.

2. Entertainment in the Evening:

When the sun sets and the ship heads into the night, the entertainment only ramps up. Here's what you can look forward to after dinner:

Live Music and Shows:

Cruise ships often feature incredible **theatrical productions**, with performances ranging from Broadway-style musicals to comedy shows and concerts. You'll also find **live music** in various lounges and bars, playing everything from jazz to pop hits, depending on the ship's theme and atmosphere. If you enjoy a more relaxed evening, you can head to the ship's **piano bar** or **lounge**, where you can enjoy a drink and listen to smooth music.

Comedy and Cabaret:

For those looking to laugh, **comedians** and **cabaret shows** are often part of the evening lineup. These performances can be lighthearted and fun, and they offer a chance to unwind after a day of exploration.

Nightlife and Clubs:

For guests who want to dance the night away, most ships have a **nightclub** or **dance floor**. Expect a lively atmosphere with a DJ or live band playing music ranging from classic hits to contemporary dance tracks. Whether you're into salsa, disco, or just casual clubbing, there's usually something happening in the evenings.

Casino and Late-Night Entertainment:

Many cruise ships have a **casino**, where you can try your luck at **blackjack**, **poker**, or the **slot machines**. Afterward, head to the ship's **late-night venue** for some snacks, drinks, and more entertainment, like karaoke or late-night comedy shows.

3. Relaxing and Wellness:

If you prefer a more laid-back day, cruise ships have a variety of relaxing activities, including:

Spas and Wellness Centers:

Most ships have **spas** offering massages, facials, and body treatments. You can book a treatment to unwind after an excursion or simply to pamper yourself. Some ships even offer **thermal suites**, which are exclusive spaces that feature saunas, hot tubs, and heated loungers, perfect for relaxing.

Library and Quiet Lounges:

For a peaceful day, head to the ship's **library** or **quiet lounges** where you can curl up with a good book, play cards, or just enjoy the serenity of the surroundings.

83 | Norwegian Fjords Cruise Travel Guide 2025

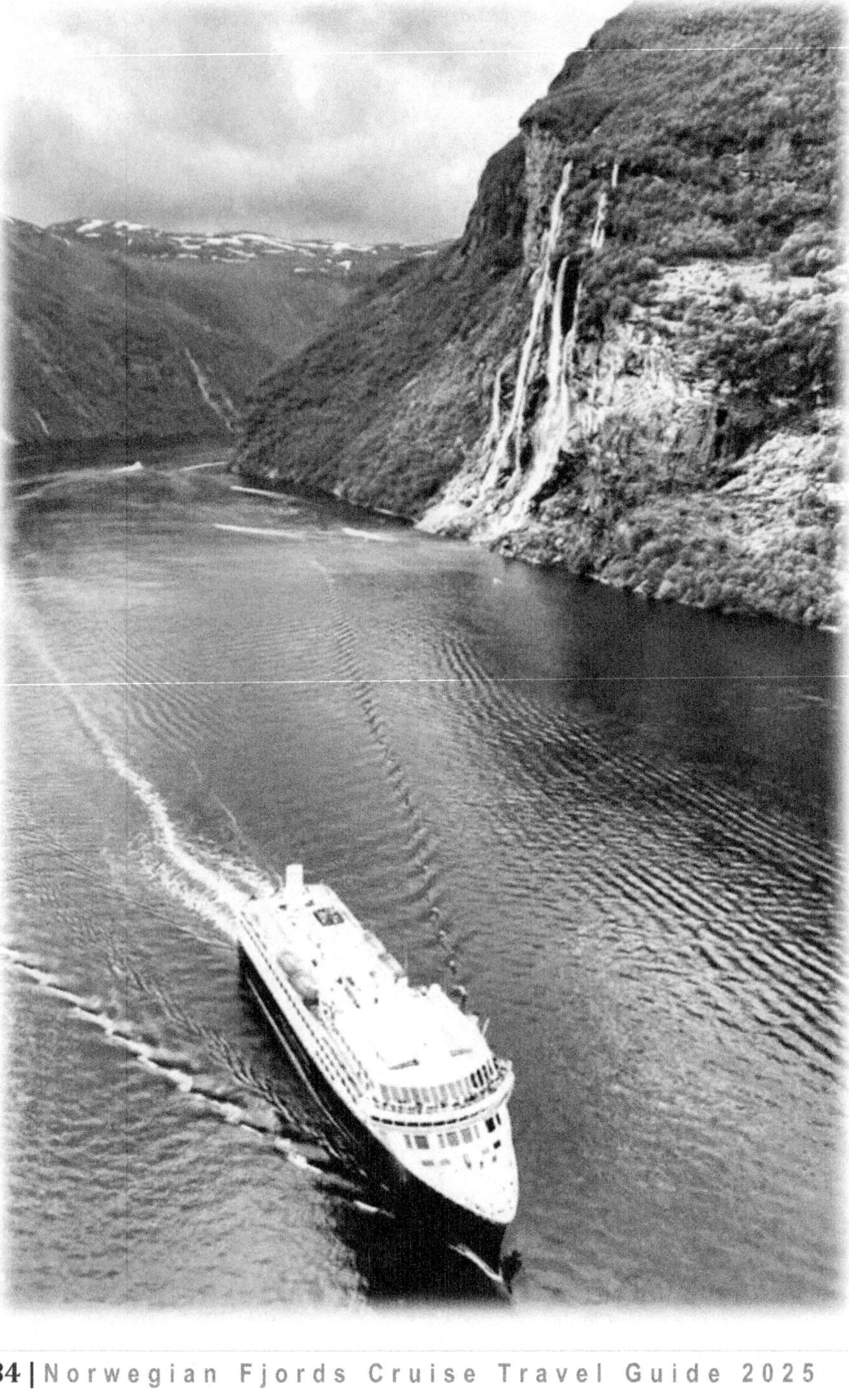

Chapter 4

Exploring Norway's Iconic Fjords and Coastal Cities

Norway's fjords and coastal cities offer some of the most breathtaking landscapes and outdoor experiences in the world. This chapter explores **Bergen**, often called the **Gateway to the Fjords**, where visitors can take the **Fløibanen Funicular** to **Mount Fløyen** for stunning city and fjord views. Nearby, **Geirangerfjord** captivates with its dramatic cliffs, waterfalls, and hiking trails, while **Ålesund** enchants with its **Art Nouveau architecture** and panoramic vistas from **Aksla Viewpoint**.

Further north, **Tromsø** offers Arctic wildlife experiences and year-round adventure, and in the heart of the fjords, **Flåm** is an outdoor enthusiast's paradise, with scenic train rides, fjord kayaking, and hiking. Finally, **Stavanger** combines coastal charm with adventure, offering thrilling fjord excursions, including hikes to **Preikestolen (Pulpit Rock)**.

This chapter details these must-visit destinations, highlighting excursions, activities, and stunning viewpoints for an unforgettable Norwegian experience.

Bergen: The Gateway to the Fjords

Bergen is often called the "Gateway to the Fjords" because it's the perfect starting point for exploring some of the most spectacular landscapes in the world. Located along Norway's southwestern coast, Bergen is not only surrounded by fjords but also steeped in history, culture, and natural beauty. Whether you're walking through its vibrant streets, visiting its famous landmarks, or embarking on a fjord cruise, Bergen offers a variety of experiences for every type of traveler.

Exploring the Bryggen Wharf

One of Bergen's most iconic and well-preserved landmarks is the **Bryggen Wharf**, a UNESCO World Heritage site that dates back to the 14th century. The Bryggen area is a maze of wooden buildings, narrow alleyways, and colorful facades, which were originally constructed by the Hanseatic merchants who traded in Bergen. Walking through these old wooden structures feels like stepping back in time, and it's a must-see for anyone visiting the city.

What to See:

Bryggen is not just a historic site—it's also home to museums, galleries, and shops. The **Bryggens Museum**

(Dreggsallmenningen 5, 5003 Bergen, Norway) showcases the history of the area, highlighting its role as a bustling trade hub in medieval times. You can also visit small shops selling **local handicrafts**, **Norwegian art**, and souvenirs. The area is lined with restaurants and cafes, where you can stop for a bite and enjoy local specialties like **klippfisk** (dried salted cod) or a comforting **Norwegian pastry**.

- **Contact**: bryggen@museum.no | +47 55 30 80 30.
- **Website**: www.bryggen.museum.no
- **Address**: Bryggens Museum, Dreggsalmenningen 3, 5003 Bergen, Norway.
- **Opening Hours**: Daily; 10:00am – 3:00pm.
- **Entry Fee**: Adults: 160 NOK | Seniors/Students: 120 NOK | Children (0–17): Free.

Guided Tours:

To make the most of your visit to Bryggen, consider joining a guided tour. Several companies offer walking tours of Bryggen, explaining the history of the buildings and the area. One such company is **I Love Bergen Walking Tour** (https://www.ilovebergen.net/), where you can book a guided tour for about 2 hours. Tours are usually available in several languages, including English.

- **Contact**: bookings@thehiddennorth.com | +47 940 54 465.
- **Website**: www.ilovebergen.net
- **Address**: Bradbenken 1, 5003 Bergen, Norway.
- **Opening Hours**: Daily; 9:00am – 3:00pm.

Visiting Mount Fløyen and the Fløibanen Funicular

Bergen is known for its dramatic scenery, and one of the best ways to experience it is by visiting **Mount Fløyen**. The mountain rises 320 meters above the city and offers panoramic views of Bergen, the fjords, and the surrounding mountains. If you're looking for a scenic way to reach the summit, the **Fløibanen Funicular** is the way to go.

What to Expect:

The *Fløibanen Funicular* (Vetrlidsallmenningen 23A, 5014 Bergen, Norway) is one of Norway's most popular attractions, carrying passengers up the mountain in just a few minutes. The ride is an experience in itself, offering fantastic views as you ascend. At the top, you'll find a variety of walking trails, viewpoints, and even a café where you can relax with a warm drink while soaking in the views. If you're feeling adventurous, you can hike back down the mountain, or simply enjoy the view from the top.

- **Contact:** info@floyen.no | +47 55 33 68 00.
- **Website**: www.floyen.no

- **Address**: Vetrlidsallmenningen 23A, 5014 Bergen, Norway.
- **Opening Hours:** Monday–Friday 07:30am – 12:00am; Saturday–Sunday 08:00am –12:00am.
- **Entry Fee:** Return ticket: Adults NOK 140; Children (4–15 years) NOK 70; Seniors (67+) NOK 100 (valid 1/1–31/3 and 1/10–31/12).

Excursion Options:

Once at the top, there are several scenic hiking routes you can take. For example, the **Lake Skomakerdiket** trail takes you through forested areas to a picturesque lake, perfect for a peaceful stroll. If you want a longer hike, the trail up to **Mount Ulriken**, another of Bergen's famous peaks, is highly recommended. You can either hike or take the **Ulriken Cable Car** from the city center to the summit.

Visiting the Fish Market

No visit to Bergen is complete without a trip to the **Fish Market**, one of the oldest and most popular open-air markets in Norway. Located right by the harbor, it's a great place to try some local seafood and experience the lively atmosphere. The market is open year-round, offering fresh fish, shellfish, fruits, vegetables, and other local goods.

What to See and Do:

Walk through the market stalls and sample fresh fish like **salmon**, **herring**, and **mussels**, or try **traditional Norwegian smoked salmon**. The Fish Market is also a great place to buy **local handicrafts** or **Norwegian wool products** as souvenirs. If you're interested in learning more about Norway's seafood industry, many market vendors are happy to share their knowledge about the fish you see on display.

- **Contact**: info@fisketorget.no | +47 55 30 48 00.
- **Website**: https://www.bergen.kommune.no/
- **Address**: Torget, 5, 5014 Bergen, Norway.
- **Opening Hours:** Monday–Thursday: 10:00–21:00| Friday–Saturday: 10:00–23:00 | Sunday: 12:00–21:00.
- **Entry Fee:** Free.

Dining at the Fish Market:

If you're hungry, there are a number of small restaurants and food stalls around the market where you can enjoy freshly prepared seafood dishes. Try the classic Norwegian dish of **fish soup**, or enjoy **crab claws** with a glass of local beer. For an unforgettable experience, you can book a **seafood tour** or

cooking class at the Fish Market, where you'll learn how to prepare dishes using the freshest ingredients.

Excursions Around Bergen

The city's main attractions, there are plenty of shore excursions that allow you to explore the surrounding area. From scenic boat trips to remote hiking trails, the options are endless.

Sognefjord Cruise:

Sognefjord is one of Norway's most famous fjords, and it's just a short boat ride from Bergen. A fjord cruise is an excellent way to witness the stunning landscape of towering cliffs, waterfalls, and picturesque villages. Several companies, including **Norway in a Nutshell** (www.norwaynutshell.com), offer guided day tours from Bergen that combine train rides, bus rides, and boat trips to take you through the fjord and its breathtaking surroundings.

Hardangerfjord Excursion:

For something a bit further afield, consider a trip to **Hardangerfjord**, another of Norway's most beautiful fjords. You can reach the fjord via bus or a scenic drive, and there are various guided tours available that take you to **Vøringsfossen**, one of Norway's most spectacular waterfalls. **Hardangerfjord Tours** (www.hardangerfjord.com) offers a range of excursions, from **boat trips** to more **adventurous hikes**.

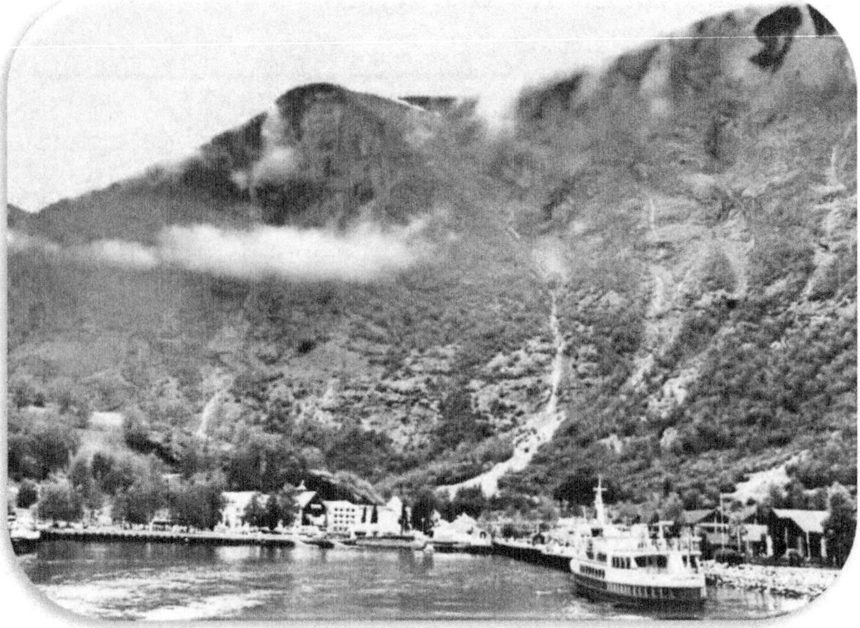

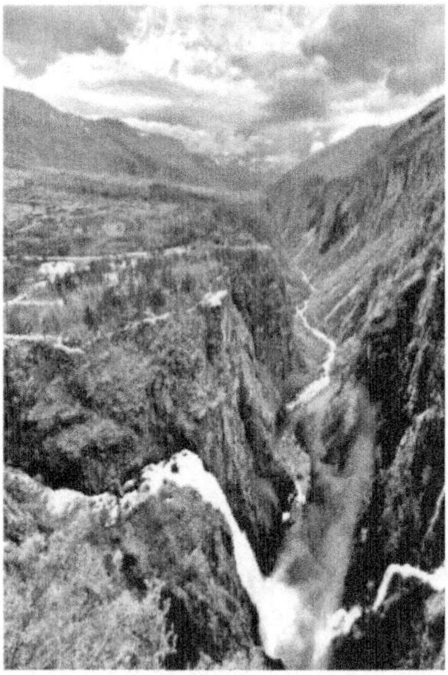

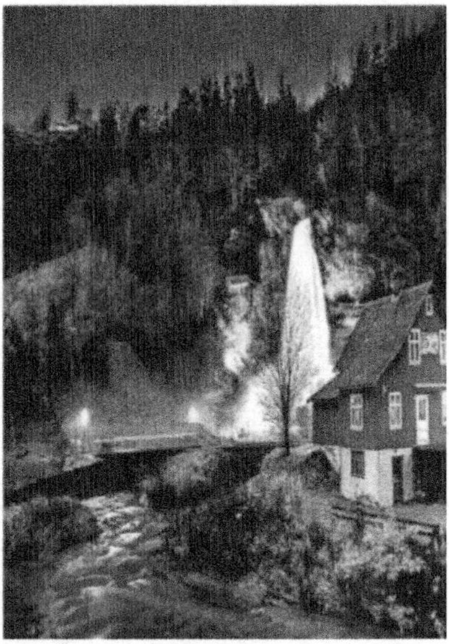

Geirangerfjord: The Jewel of the Fjords

Geirangerfjord is often referred to as the most beautiful fjord in the world, and it's easy to see why. This UNESCO World Heritage site is a breathtaking masterpiece, where towering cliffs rise dramatically from the crystal-clear waters below. The fjord is dotted with lush green landscapes, cascading waterfalls, and picturesque villages, creating a scenery that's simply beyond compare. Exploring *Geirangerfjord* is a must on any Norwegian Fjords cruise, and there's so much to do and see once you arrive.

Scenic Views from Dalsnibba

One of the best ways to take in the spectacular beauty of **Geirangerfjord** is by visiting **Dalsnibba**, a mountain peak that offers panoramic views of the fjord and the surrounding landscapes. Located 1,500 meters above sea level, *Dalsnibba* is one of the highest viewpoints accessible by road in Norway, and it provides an unforgettable perspective of the fjord's deep blue waters and snow-capped mountains.

What to Expect:

The road up to Dalsnibba is an adventure in itself. The **Geiranger Skywalk** road winds its way up the mountain, offering increasingly breathtaking views as you climb. Once at the summit, you'll be treated to sweeping views of Geirangerfjord, with towering cliffs and dramatic landscapes stretching out in every direction. The **Dalsnibba Viewpoint** is equipped with a **platform** that lets you stand above the fjord, looking down at the tiny village of Geiranger far below. It's the perfect spot for photos, and the clarity of the air and the sheer beauty of the surroundings make it a magical experience.

Excursion Options:

Several companies offer guided tours to Dalsnibba, which include transportation to and from the viewpoint, along with explanations about the area's history and geography. For instance, **Geiranger Fjordservice** offers bus tours that take you up to Dalsnibba, giving you time to soak in the views and take pictures before heading back down.

Ticket Information:

A ticket for the **Geiranger Skywalk** can be purchased either at the viewing platform or online through the official website. Tickets typically cost around **200 NOK** for adults. The journey to Dalsnibba is often combined with a visit to other local attractions, such as the **Eagle Road**, another scenic route with stunning views of the fjord.

Contact Information:

- **Contact**: booking@dalsnibba.no | +47 45 48 13 01.

- **Website**: www.dalsnibba.no

- **Address**: Dalsnibba Viewpoint, 6216 Geiranger, Norway.

- **Opening Hours:** Toll road open 24 hours, May–October. Shop and café: May–June 14: 09:30–17:00; June 15–August 15: 09:30–18:00; August 16–September: 09:30–16:30.

- **Entry Fee:** Motorbike: NOK 170; Car: NOK 330; Bus: NOK 2,830.

Hiking and Waterfalls

Geirangerfjord is not just for scenic drives—it's also a paradise for hikers and nature lovers. The fjord is surrounded by several hiking trails that lead you through lush forests, along cliffsides, and to some of the area's most iconic waterfalls. Whether you're looking for an easy walk or a more challenging hike, there are plenty of options to explore this remarkable part of Norway.

What to Expect:

One of the most famous hikes is the **Seven Sisters Waterfall Hike**, which takes you along a trail that leads to the base of the Seven Sisters Waterfall. This stunning waterfall is made up of seven separate streams, each cascading down the mountainside into the fjord below. The hike offers incredible views of the waterfall as well as the surrounding fjord and mountains. The walk is relatively easy, making it accessible to most visitors, though there are some steep sections.

Hiking Trails:

There are also more challenging hikes in the area for those looking to push themselves. The **Bendiksdal** and **Mt. Slogen** trails offer more demanding treks, with steep ascents and breathtaking views. The **Bendiksdal trail** takes you through forests and offers a panoramic view of the fjord once you reach the summit. For experienced hikers, the **Mt. Slogen** trail provides a truly challenging ascent with rewarding views at the top. These hikes should be attempted by those who are comfortable with steep, rocky terrain.

Guided Hikes:

If you prefer a guided experience, several companies offer hiking tours around Geirangerfjord. **Geiranger Fjordservice** provides guided hikes to several waterfalls, including the Seven Sisters, where an expert guide will lead you and share insights about the landscape, flora, and fauna of the region.

Waterfall Tours:

If hiking is not your preference, there are also boat tours that take you to the base of Geirangerfjord's famous waterfalls. These boat tours offer a relaxing way to view the falls, with the option to hop off at various points and take short walks to get closer to the waterfalls.

Contact Information:

- **Contact**: booking@geirangerfjord.no | +47 70 26 30 07.
- **Website**: www.geirangerfjord.no
- **Address**: Geirangerfjordservice AS, Geiranger, Norway.

- **Opening Hours:** Monday–Sunday: 09:00–17:00.
- **Estimated Fee:** From NOK 530.

Contact for Hiking Tours:

For guided hikes, you can also contact **Geiranger Adventures**, which offers customized tours for all levels of hikers.

Contact Information:

- **Contact**: info@geirangeradventures.no | +47 70 26 30 07.
- **Website**: www.geiranger-adventure.no
- **Address**: Geirangervegen 10, 6216 Geiranger, Norway.
- **Estimated Fee**: Prices vary by activity; for example, a 3-hour guided kayak tour costs approximately NOK 1,200 per person.

Additional Information

When to Visit Geirangerfjord:

The best time to visit Geirangerfjord is during the summer months, from June to August, when the weather is mild, and most of the attractions and hiking trails are fully accessible. However, if you're interested in seeing the fjord covered in snow and experiencing a quieter, more serene atmosphere, visiting in late spring or early autumn can be a fantastic option.

Getting There:

If you're arriving via cruise, Geirangerfjord is easily accessible from the port. However, if you're traveling independently, the **Eagle Road** offers a spectacular drive into Geiranger from the nearby town of **Ørnes**, about 45 minutes away by car.

GEIRANGERFJORD

SCAN THE QR CODE

102 | Norwegian Fjords Cruise Travel Guide 2025

Alesund: Art Nouveau and Panoramic Views

Alesund is often described as one of the most picturesque towns in Norway, and it's easy to see why. Nestled between the mountains and the sea, Alesund is famous for its distinctive **Art Nouveau architecture**, scenic waterfront, and sweeping panoramic views. Whether you're walking through the charming streets or taking in the views from the hills above, there's something magical about this town that makes it a must-visit destination on your Norwegian Fjords cruise.

Discovering the Town's Architecture

Alesund is renowned for its **Art Nouveau architecture**, which gives the town a unique and cohesive aesthetic. The town was rebuilt in the early 1900s after a devastating fire, and the new buildings were designed in a style that blended elements of **Art Nouveau** with traditional Norwegian designs. The result is a town that feels like a work of art, with flowing lines, vibrant colors, and intricate details adorning the facades of buildings.

What to Expect:

As you stroll through Alesund, you'll notice the whimsical, yet sophisticated style of its buildings. **Curved corners**, **floral motifs**, and **ornate stonework** are a common feature of the town's architecture, and the pastel hues of the buildings make Alesund feel bright and welcoming. The town's **center** is compact and easy to explore on foot, so take your time as you wander through the streets and alleyways, admiring the unique designs.

- **Key Buildings to See**:
- The **Alesund Town Hall**, located in the heart of the city, is a prime example of Art Nouveau architecture, featuring beautiful windows and decorative elements.
- The **Kongsplassen**, or King's Square, is home to several striking buildings, with some dating back to the early 1900s.
- Another iconic building is the **Jugendstilsenteret**, which is dedicated to the Art Nouveau movement. Housed in a beautiful building, the center offers insight into the architecture and history of Alesund's design.

Guided Tours:

For a deeper understanding of the town's unique architecture, consider booking a **walking tour** with **Alesund Tourist Information**. They offer guided tours that delve into the history and design of the buildings. The tours typically last 1-2 hours, and you'll have the chance to hear about the **fire of 1904**, which led to the reconstruction of the town in the Art Nouveau style.

Contact Information:

- **Contact**: info@visitalesund.com | +47 70 15 76 00.

- **Website**: www.visitalesund.com

- **Address**: Skateflukaia, 6002 Ålesund, Norway.

- **Opening Hours:** Monday–Friday: 08:30AM–4:00PM; Saturday–Sunday: Closed.

The Aksla Viewpoint

One of the best ways to appreciate Alesund's unique setting is from **Aksla Viewpoint**, a hilltop that offers panoramic views of the town, the surrounding islands, and the **Alesund Peninsula**. The viewpoint is located just a short distance from the town center and provides the perfect spot for capturing those stunning photographs of Alesund.

What to Expect:

The **Aksla Viewpoint** is reached via a steep climb of 418 steps, known as the **Aksla Steps**, or you can take a **short drive** or **bus ride** to the summit. Once you reach the top, the views are absolutely worth the effort. From this vantage point, you can see the picturesque town with its art-deco-style buildings nestled by the fjord, surrounded by rugged mountains and the open sea. On a clear day, the scenery stretches for miles, and the beauty is nothing short of breathtaking.

What to Do:

At the viewpoint, you'll find **benches** where you can sit and take in the views, and there's also a **café** where you can enjoy a warm drink while overlooking the fjord. The **Aksla Viewpoint** is especially popular for sunset, when the town lights up and the water takes on a golden hue.

Hiking Options:

For the more adventurous, the viewpoint also serves as a starting point for several hiking trails, including paths that lead through the forests and up the mountainsides. Whether you're looking for a **short walk** or a **longer hike**, Aksla is a great place to connect with nature and enjoy the serenity of the surrounding landscapes.

Guided Tours:

If you'd prefer to have a guide, **Hop-on Hop-off sightseeing Alesund** offers trips to **Aksla Viewpoint** as part of their package, where you'll not only get to enjoy the view but also learn about the history of the town and its landmarks.

Contact Information:

- **Contact**: info@hopon.no | +47 70 12 58 04.

- **Website**: www.hopon.no

- **Address**: Cruise Terminal, Keiser Wilhelms g. 6, 6003 Ålesund, Norway.

- **Opening Hours:** Monday–Sunday: 9:00 AM–4:00 PM.

Additional Information

When to Visit Alesund:

Alesund is a year-round destination, with each season offering something special. During the summer months (June to August), the town is bustling with life, and the weather is ideal for sightseeing. Autumn (September to October) brings vibrant foliage, making it the perfect time for photography. In winter, Alesund has a magical feel, with fewer tourists and the chance to experience the town covered in snow.

Getting Around Alesund:

The town itself is very compact, making it easy to explore on foot. If you're looking to visit the **Aksla Viewpoint** or other attractions located further out of town, you can use the local **public buses**, or opt for a **taxi** or **bike rental** for a more personal experience. Many cruise lines also offer shore excursions that include transportation to and from Alesund's main sights.

Shore Excursions:

Alesund is a popular stop for many Norwegian Fjords cruises, so there are plenty of excursions available. From guided walking tours to scenic boat trips, there's a lot to see and do. For those interested in nature, excursions to nearby islands or fjords are a fantastic way to explore the region further.

Popular Excursion Companies:

- **Alesund Shore Excursions**: www.visitalesund.com
- **Hurtigruten Excursions**: www.hurtigruten.com
- **Geiranger Fjordservice**: www.geirangerfjord.no

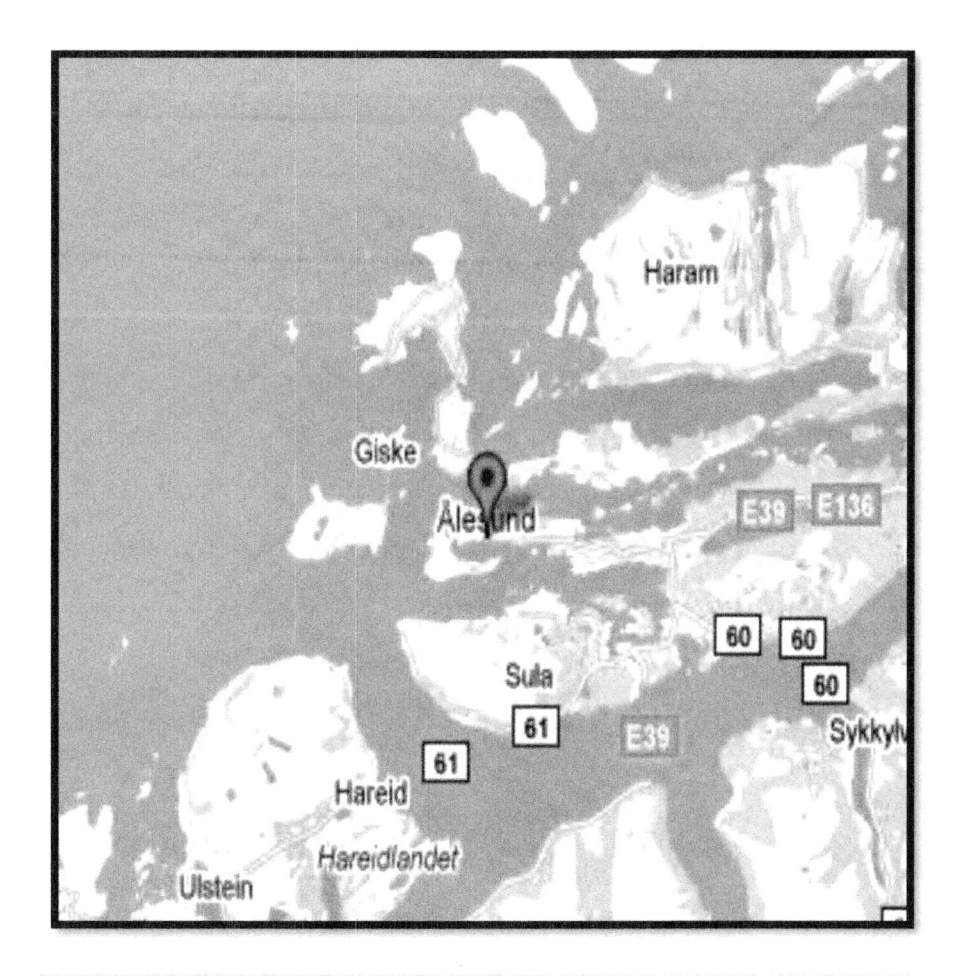

Tromsø: Gateway to the Arctic

Tromsø, often referred to as the **Gateway to the Arctic**, is a city that sits above the Arctic Circle, offering travelers a chance to experience both the extremes of nature and the wonders of the Arctic environment. With its spectacular views, rich cultural heritage, and thrilling outdoor activities, Tromsø has become one of Norway's most exciting destinations, especially for those looking to explore the northernmost regions of the world.

Northern Lights Viewing (Seasonal)

One of Tromsø's main attractions is its reputation as one of the best places in the world to see the **Northern Lights**. Every year, thousands of travelers' flock to Tromsø hoping to catch a glimpse of this incredible natural phenomenon. The Northern Lights, or **Aurora Borealis**, are a spectacular light display caused by solar particles interacting with Earth's magnetic field, and Tromsø's position above the Arctic Circle makes it one of the most reliable places to witness this magical event.

What to Expect:

The best time to see the Northern Lights in Tromsø is from **late September to early April**. During these months, the skies are darkest, providing ideal conditions for viewing. You can often see the Northern Lights from the city itself, but for the best experience, many visitors choose to book a **guided Northern Lights tour** that takes them away from the light pollution of the city and into more remote areas.

How to See the Northern Lights:

You can choose to go on a **chasing tour**, where experienced guides take you out in search of the best possible viewing conditions. These tours typically last 5-7 hours and may take you into surrounding areas like the Lyngen Alps or nearby islands, where the Northern Lights can often be seen in all their glory. You'll likely have a chance to stop for hot drinks and snacks while waiting for the aurora to appear, as the phenomenon can be unpredictable. The **Northern Lights** are best viewed in the **dark hours of the night**, typically between 10 p.m. and 2 a.m.

Contact for Northern Lights Tours:

For booking Northern Lights tours, one of the most reputable companies in Tromsø is **Chasing Lights** (info@chasinglights.com | +47 95 22 15 55). They offer guided tours with photographers, so you can capture the Northern Lights in the best possible way.

Ticket Information:

Prices for a Northern Lights tour typically range from **1,200 NOK to 1,600 NOK** per person, depending on the tour duration and inclusions. It's recommended to book in advance, especially during the peak winter months when tours fill up quickly.

Contact Information for Northern Lights Viewing:

- **Contact**: info@chasinglights.com | +47 92 29 15 55.
- **Website**: www.chasinglights.com
- **Address**: Tromsø Tourist Information, Storgata 64A, 9008 Tromsø, Norway.

Arctic Wildlife and Activities

Tromsø is also known for its incredible wildlife and range of **Arctic activities**. Whether you're interested in seeing Arctic animals up close, experiencing the region's stunning landscapes, or getting your adrenaline pumping with outdoor activities, Tromsø has something for everyone.

Whale Watching:

Tromsø is a prime location for **whale watching**, particularly from November to January when **humpback whales** and **orcas** migrate through the waters surrounding the city. There are several boat tours available that take you out on the fjords to spot these majestic creatures.

The tours typically last 3-5 hours and often provide knowledgeable guides who will help you spot whales, seals, and even sea eagles. One company that offers excellent whale-watching tours is **Arctic Wild Tours** (www.arcticwild.no | +47 99 55 31 31). They offer both small group and private tours to increase your chances of spotting whales.

Dog Sledding:

For an authentic Arctic experience, **dog sledding** is a must-do activity. In Tromsø, you can embark on a **dog sledding adventure** through snow-covered landscapes with a team of friendly sled dogs. These tours allow you to drive your own sled or be driven by an experienced guide. The experience is both thrilling and serene, and it gives you the chance to see the beauty of the Arctic wilderness up close. Popular providers like **Arctic Adventure Tours** (www.arcticadventuretours.no | +47 45 63 52 88) offer half-day and full-day dog sledding trips.

Snowmobiling:

If you're looking for more adventure, **snowmobiling** in the Arctic is another exhilarating option. Tromsø offers several snowmobile tours, where you can race across frozen landscapes, fjords, and glaciers. One recommended provider is **Arctic Safari** (www.arcticsafari.no | +47 91 80 94 75), which offers snowmobile safaris that take you to remote areas with spectacular views of the surrounding mountains and fjords.

Other Activities:

In addition to wildlife watching, dog sledding, and snowmobiling, Tromsø offers plenty of other activities, such as **cross-country skiing**, **ice fishing**, and **hiking** in the surrounding mountains. During the summer months, you can also go **kayaking** in the fjords or take part in a **midnight sun cruise**.

Contact Information for Arctic Activities:

Whale Watching Tours:

- o   **Contact**: info@arcticwildtours.com | +47 99 55 31 31.

- o   **Website**: www.arcticwildtours.com

- o   **Address**: Løkkeveien 4, 9008 Tromsø, Norway.

- o   **Opening Hours:** Monday-Sunday: 9:00 AM - 4:00 PM.

- o   **Price Range:** Varies by tour; for example, the Arctic Nature Tour is priced at about 1,200 NOK per person.

Dog Sledding Tours:

- o   **Contact**: post@arcticadventuretours.no | +47 45 63 52 88.

- o   **Website**: www.arcticadventuretours.no.

- o   **Address**: Straumsvegen 993, 9109 Kvaløya, Tromsø, Norway.

- o   **Opening Hours:** Monday–Friday: 08:00AM–5PM.

- o   **Price Range:** Prices vary by activity; for example, self-drive husky dog sledding is around 4,700 NOK per person.

Snowmobiling Tours:

- **Contact**: morten@arcticsafari.no | +47 91 80 94 75.
- **Website**: www.tromsosafari.no
- **Address**: Conrad Holmboes veg 53, 9011 Tromsø, Norway.
- **Opening Hours:** Daily, at all hours.

Additional Information

When to Visit Tromsø:

The best time to visit Tromsø for the **Northern Lights** is during the winter months, from **November to March.** This is when the town experiences the darkest nights and the best opportunities to witness the Northern Lights. For those interested in Arctic wildlife or outdoor activities like dog sledding and snowmobiling, the winter months are also ideal. If you prefer the **Midnight Sun**, Tromsø offers 24 hours of daylight from **late May to mid-July**, which is another magical experience to witness in this Arctic region.

Getting Around Tromsø:

Tromsø is a small, walkable city, but for reaching more remote attractions or excursions, you can take advantage of **public**

transport, taxis, or **guided tours**. Many of the activity providers offer pick-up and drop-off services at your hotel or the cruise port, making it easier to get to your destination.

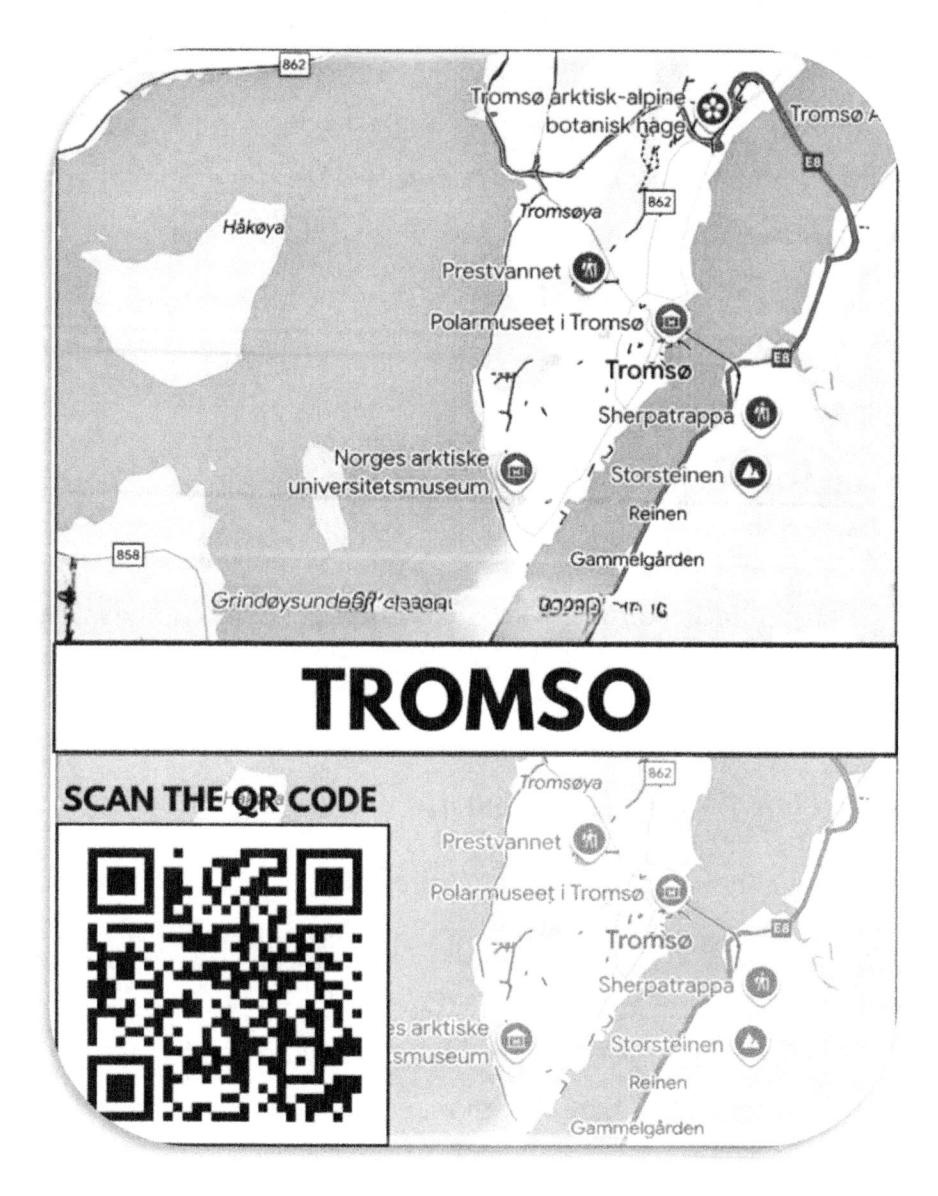

Flåm: The Heart of the Fjords

Flåm, a small village nestled at the innermost point of the Aurlandsfjord, is one of the most sought-after destinations in Norway, offering visitors an unparalleled combination of **stunning natural beauty**, **rich cultural heritage**, and an array of **outdoor adventures**. Located in the **Sogn og Fjordane** region, Flåm has become a popular stop on the Norwegian fjords cruise route, attracting travelers who want to explore the very best of Norway's rugged landscapes.

Top Attractions in Flåm

Flåm is not only known for its breathtaking fjord views but also for its **iconic landmarks**, **world-class experiences**, and **memorable outdoor activities**. Here's a comprehensive guide to what you can do and see while in Flåm:

The Flåm Railway (Flåmsbana)

A highlight of any visit to Flåm is the **Flåm Railway**, often hailed as one of the most scenic train journeys in the world. This 20-kilometer route travels from **Flåm** to **Myrdal**, climbing over 800 meters through **hairpin bends**, **lush valleys**, and **waterfalls**. The journey offers a unique perspective of the fjord landscape, showcasing Norway's rugged beauty. The train ride also includes a stop at **Kjosfossen**, where you can witness the thunderous waterfall up close. Tickets for the Flåm Railway can be booked in advance through the official website.

- **Contact:** info@flamsbana.no | +47 57 63 21 00.
- **Website:** www.flamsbana.no
- **Address:** Flåm, 5743 Aurland, Norway.
- **Opening Hours:** Monday - Sunday: 8:00 AM - 5:00 PM.
- **Price Range:** From 430 NOK per person for a one-way ticket.

Nærøyfjord Cruise

The **Nærøyfjord**, a UNESCO World Heritage Site, is known for its narrow and dramatic nature, surrounded by towering cliffs and cascading waterfalls. Visitors can take a **boat cruise** from Flåm to **Gudvangen**, passing through one of the most spectacular fjords in the world.

- **Contact**: info@naeroyfjord.no | +47 57 63 00 00.
- **Website:** www.naroyfjord.no
- **Address:** Flåm, 5742 Flåm, Norway.
- **Duration**: Approximately 2 hours.

- **Price Range:** Approximately 590 NOK per person.

Stegastein Viewpoint

For panoramic views of **Aurlandsfjord**, **Stegastein Viewpoint** is a must-visit. Located 650 meters above sea level, the viewpoint offers stunning vistas of the fjord below, with its curving waters and lush forests. The platform is designed to extend out from the cliff, allowing visitors to experience breathtaking views in every direction. It is accessible by car, bus, or as part of a guided tour, and it is an excellent spot for photography.

- **Contact:** info@stegastein.no
- **Website:** https://www.visitnorway.com/
- **Address:** Bjørgavegen, 83, 5743 Aurland, Norway.
- **Opening Hours:** Open year-round, accessible at all hours.
- **Price Range:** Free entry.

Viking Valley in Gudvangen

For those looking to dive into Norwegian history, **Viking Valley** in **Gudvangen** is a short drive away from Flåm. This open-air museum offers visitors the chance to step back in time and experience **Viking culture** firsthand. The site includes reconstructed Viking longhouses, ancient crafts, and opportunities to participate in Viking-themed activities. Guided tours offer a comprehensive look at the history and traditions of the Viking Age.

- **Contact:** info@vikingvalley.no | +47 46 23 54 62.
- **Website:** www.vikingvalley.no
- **Address:** Gudvangen, 5747 Aurland, Norway.
- **Opening Hours:** Monday-Sunday: 10:30 AM - 2:00 PM.
- **Entry Fee:** From 250 NOK per person for entrance.

Flåm Church (Flåm Kyrkje)

This small, yet **beautiful wooden church** is a serene place to visit. Built in 1670, it is a fine example of **traditional Norwegian church architecture**, with intricate woodwork and lovely stained-glass windows. It's also one of the oldest wooden churches in the region.

- **Contact:** info@flam.com
- **Website:** https://www.norske-kirker.net/

- **Address:** Ryavegen 5, 5743 Flam, Norway.

- **Opening Hours:** Monday-Sunday: 9:00 AM - 5:00 PM (Seasonal).

- **Entry Fee:** Free, but donations are appreciated.

Outdoor Activities in Flåm

Flåm offers a wide range of outdoor activities, from **hiking** to **kayaking**. Here are some exciting adventures you can enjoy during your visit:

Hiking Trails

Flåm is a haven for nature lovers and hikers. The region has several **scenic hiking trails** that range from easy walks to more challenging treks.

- **Aurlandsdalen Valley**: A **popular hiking route** known as "Norway's Grand Canyon", with **spectacular landscapes**.
- **Rallarvegen**: An iconic **mountain biking trail** that follows an old construction road, offering **stunning views** of the fjord and surrounding landscapes.

Recommended Operator (FjordSafari):

- **Contact**: post@fjordsafari.com | +47 57 63 33 23.
- **Website**: https://www.fjordsafari.com/
- **Address**: Inner harbor Flåm center, 5742 Flåm, Norway.
- **Opening Hours:** Monday - Sunday: 8:00 AM - 9:00 PM.

- **Price Range:** Approximately NOK 650 - NOK 1,060 per person, depending on the tour selected.

Kayaking and Fjord Paddling

For a more intimate experience with the fjords, consider taking a **kayak tour** through the serene waters of **Aurlandsfjord** or **Nærøyfjord**. These guided paddling tours allow you to explore the fjords at your own pace and get closer to the waterfalls and natural wonders.

Recommended Operator (Nordic Ventures AS):

- **Contact**: info@nordicventures.com | +47 56 51 00 17.
- **Website**: www.nordicventures.com
- **Address**: Sea Kayak Center Gudvangen, 5747, Norway.
- **Opening Hours:** Monday - Sunday: 8:00 AM - 5:00 PM.
- **Price Range:** Approximately NOK 895 – NOK 39,995 per person, depending on the tour selected.

Cycling the Rallarvegen

Rallarvegen is one of Norway's most popular biking routes, winding through **stunning landscapes** from Flåm to the top of the mountains. The route offers spectacular **views of glaciers**, **waterfalls**, and **fjords**.

Recommended Operator (Visit Norway):

- **Contact:** info@visitnorway.com | +47 23 28 29 00.
- **Website:** www.visitnorway.com
- **Address:** Grev Wedels plass 9, 0151 Oslo, Norway
- **Opening Hours:** Monday–Friday: 08:00AM – 4:00PM.

Getting to Flåm:

Flåm is easily accessible by **train**, **bus**, and **car**. The Flåm Railway connects Flåm to **Myrdal**, where you can transfer to other railway lines, making it easy to get to and from the village. If you're arriving from **Bergen**, you can take the **Bergen Railway** to **Voss**, and then transfer to a bus that will take you to Flåm. **Cruise ships** also dock in Flåm, making it a popular stop on your Norwegian fjord cruise.

When to Visit Flåm:

The best time to visit Flåm depends on the experience you want. **Summer** (June to August) is ideal for outdoor activities like hiking, biking, and enjoying the long days of the **Midnight Sun**. For those wishing to see the **Northern Lights**, the winter months (November to March) offer the best conditions, with the town surrounded by snow-capped mountains and frozen fjords.

Flåm

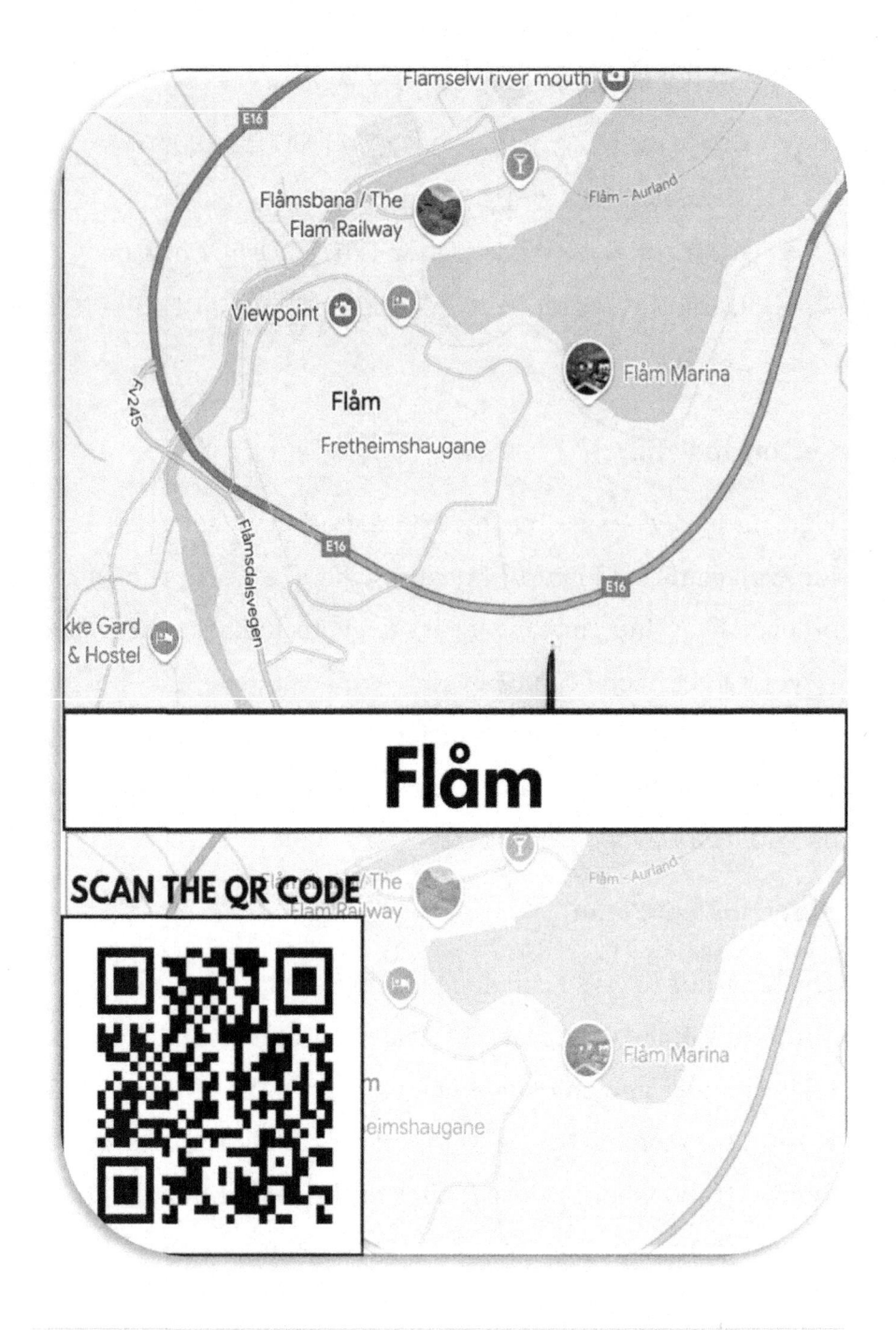

SCAN THE QR CODE

Stavanger: Norway's Coastal Gem

Stavanger, located on the southwestern coast of Norway, is a **dynamic** and historic city that serves as a major gateway to some of the country's most **breathtaking natural landscapes**. While it has deep **Viking roots and maritime history**, it is also a modern hub for culture, cuisine, and outdoor adventure. Stavanger is best known for being the starting point to some of Norway's **most iconic natural wonders**, including the world-famous **Pulpit Rock (Preikestolen)** and **Lysefjord**. Whether you're exploring the city's charming **old town**, visiting world-class museums, or setting off on an **unforgettable fjord excursion**, Stavanger offers a perfect blend of **history, adventure, and scenic beauty**.

Exploring Stavanger's Historic & Cultural Landmarks

Despite its reputation as a launch point for fjord adventures, Stavanger itself has **plenty to offer**. The city's streets are lined with **white wooden houses, cobbled alleys, and vibrant street art**, making it one of the **most picturesque towns in Norway**. Here's a comprehensive guide to what you can do and see while in Stavanger:

Gamle Stavanger: A Walk Through the Past

Gamle Stavanger, or **Old Stavanger**, is one of the best-preserved historic districts in Norway. It consists of **173 white wooden houses**, built in the 18th and 19th centuries, giving visitors a glimpse into the city's past.

What to See in Gamle Stavanger:

- Cobblestone streets lined with beautifully restored wooden homes.
- Local art galleries and boutique shops showcasing Norwegian crafts.
- The **Norwegian Canning Museum**, which tells the story of Stavanger's fishing industry.
- A peaceful and photogenic atmosphere, perfect for a **leisurely stroll**.

Contact Information for Historical Tours:

- **Contact:** info@visitnorway.com | +47 23 28 29 00.
- **Website:** www.visitnorway.com
- **Address:** Grev Wedels plass 9, 0151 Oslo, Norway
- **Opening Hours:** Monday–Friday: 08:00AM – 4:00PM.
- **Entry Fee:** Free entry (museum entrance starts at **100 NOK per person**).

Norwegian Petroleum Museum: A Unique Insight into Norway's Oil Industry

Unlike most Norwegian cities, Stavanger has become one of the **country's** wealthiest cities due to its oil industry. The **Norwegian Petroleum Museum** explains Norway's journey from a small fishing economy to a global oil powerhouse.

What to Expect:

- Interactive exhibits explaining how oil is extracted from the North Sea.
- A **simulator experience** where you can try being an offshore worker.
- Displays on energy sustainability and Norway's future in renewable energy.
- Life-sized oil rig models and simulations.
- Hands-on exhibits for kids, including a rescue chute from an oil platform.

Contact Information for the Norwegian Petroleum Museum:

- **Contact:** post@norskolje.museum.no | +47 51 93 93 00.
- **Website:** www.norskolje.museum.no
- **Address:** Kjeringholmen 1A, 4006 Stavanger, Norway.
- **Opening Hours:** Monday–Sunday: 10:00 AM – 4:00 PM.
- **Entry Fee: 150 NOK per adult**, discounts for students and children.

Sverd i Fjell (Swords in Rock) – A Monument to Viking History

Located just outside Stavanger, **Sverd i Fjell (Swords in Rock)** is a **striking Viking monument** featuring **three massive swords** embedded in the ground. This site commemorates the **Battle of Hafrsfjord (872 AD)**, where **King Harald Fairhair** united Norway into one kingdom.

What to Expect:

- A **scenic coastal setting** perfect for photography.
- An **important historical landmark** for Viking enthusiasts.
- A nearby **beach and picnic area**, great for relaxing.

Contact Information for Historical Tours and Guide:

- **Contact:** info@visitnorway.com | +47 23 28 29 00.
- **Website:** www.visitnorway.com
- **Address:** Grev Wedels plass 9, 0151 Oslo, Norway
- **Opening Hours:** Monday–Friday: 08:00AM – 4:00PM.
- **Entry Fee:** Free.

Fjord Adventures & Outdoor Activities in Stavanger

While the city itself is full of history and charm, **Stavanger is best known as a launch point for some of Norway's most famous outdoor experiences**. The region surrounding Stavanger is filled with **dramatic fjords, towering cliffs, and scenic hiking trails**, making it a **dream destination for nature lovers and adventure seekers**.

Preikestolen (Pulpit Rock) – Norway's Most Famous Hike

One of Norway's most **iconic landmarks, Preikestolen (Pulpit Rock)** is a massive cliff that towers **604 meters (1,982 feet) above the Lysefjord**. This sheer rock formation is a must-visit for adventure seekers, offering a **breathtaking panoramic view** of the fjord below.

What to Expect:

- The **hike to Preikestolen** is about **4 km (2.5 miles) each way** and takes **4-5 hours round trip**.
- The trail is well-marked but involves some **steep and uneven terrain**, so proper hiking gear is recommended.

- The best time to visit is from **May to September**, when the weather is most favorable.
- At the summit, visitors are rewarded with a **jaw-dropping panoramic view** of the fjord below.
- Many guided tours include transportation from Stavanger to the **Preikestolen Mountain Lodge**, the starting point for the hike.

How to Get There:

- Take a ferry from **Stavanger to Tau**, followed by a **bus to the Preikestolen parking area**.
- Alternatively, many companies offer **direct transportation** and guided hikes.

Guided Hike Tours:

For those who prefer an organized experience, local tour companies offer guided hikes, including **sunrise and winter hikes** with crampons. One recommended provider is **Pulpit Rock Tours**.

Contact Information for Preikestolen Hikes:

- **Contact:** preikestolen@boreal.no | +47 515 99 060.
- **Website:** www.pulpitrock.no
- **Address:** Treskeveien 5, 4043 Hafrsfjord, Norway.

- **Opening Hours:** Monday–Sunday
- **Price Range:** Adult round-trip tickets start from approximately 399 NOK.

Lysefjord Cruises: Exploring Norway's Wild Beauty

Lysefjord is a **42-km-long fjord** surrounded by **steep cliffs, waterfalls, and picturesque villages**. The best way to experience this natural wonder is by taking a **fjord cruise** or a **kayaking tour**.

Highlights of a Lysefjord Cruise:

- Up-close views of Pulpit Rock from the water.
- The stunning **Hengjanefossen Waterfall**, cascading **400 meters down**.
- **Fantahålå (Vagabond's Cave)**, a historic hideout for outlaws.
- Wildlife sightings, including **seals, eagles, and porpoises**.

Cruise Options:

- **Regular sightseeing cruises** operate from Stavanger's harbor and last about **3 hours**.

- **RIB (Rigid Inflatable Boat) safaris** offer a more adventurous experience.
- **Kayak excursions** allow for a more immersive way to experience the fjord.

Contact Information for Lysefjord Cruises (Rodne Fjord Cruise):

- **Contact:** post@rodne.no | +47 51 89 52 70.
- **Website:** www.rodne.no
- **Address:** Strandkaien 37, 4005 Stavanger, Norway.
- **Opening Hours:** Monday-Friday: 8:00 AM - 3:30 PM.
- **Entry Fee:** Standard cruise are priced from approximately **650 NOK per person**.

Sola Beach: A Coastal Escape Near Stavanger

For those looking for a relaxing break from sightseeing, **Sola Beach (Solastranden)** is one of Norway's most beautiful sandy beaches, stretching 2.3 km along the coastline near Stavanger. Known for its golden sand dunes, clear waters, and dramatic North Sea waves, it is a popular spot for **surfing, kiteboarding, and sunbathing**.

Highlights of Sola Beach?

- **Long, sandy shoreline** perfect for sunbathing, beach walks, and picnics.
- **Great conditions for water sports**, including surfing, windsurfing, and kitesurfing.
- **Scenic sunset views** over the North Sea, making it a great photography location.
- **Historical sites nearby**, including World War II bunkers and Sola Ruins Church.
- **Family-friendly** with shallow waters in some areas, ideal for kids.

Activities at Sola Beach:

- **Swimming and sunbathing** during the summer months.
- **Surfing and kitesurfing**, with rental shops and surf schools available.
- **Coastal hiking and jogging** along scenic trails.
- **Photography opportunities**, especially at sunrise and sunset.
- **Exploring the nearby Sola Ruins Church**, a medieval site dating back to the 12th century.

Contact Information for Sola Beach:

- **Contact:** info@regionstavanger.com | +47 51 85 92 00.
- **Website:** www.regionstavanger.com
- **Address:** Solastranden, 4050 Sola, Norway.
- **Opening Hours:** Open 24/7.
- **Entry Fee:** Free to visit.

Best Time to Visit Stavanger

- **Summer (June-August):** Best for hiking, fjord cruises, and exploring the city's outdoor attractions.
- **Spring/Autumn (April-May & September-October):** Great for fewer crowds and mild weather.
- **Winter (November-March):** Not ideal for hiking but offers a quieter experience with cozy cafés and museums.

137 | Norwegian Fjords Cruise Travel Guide 2025

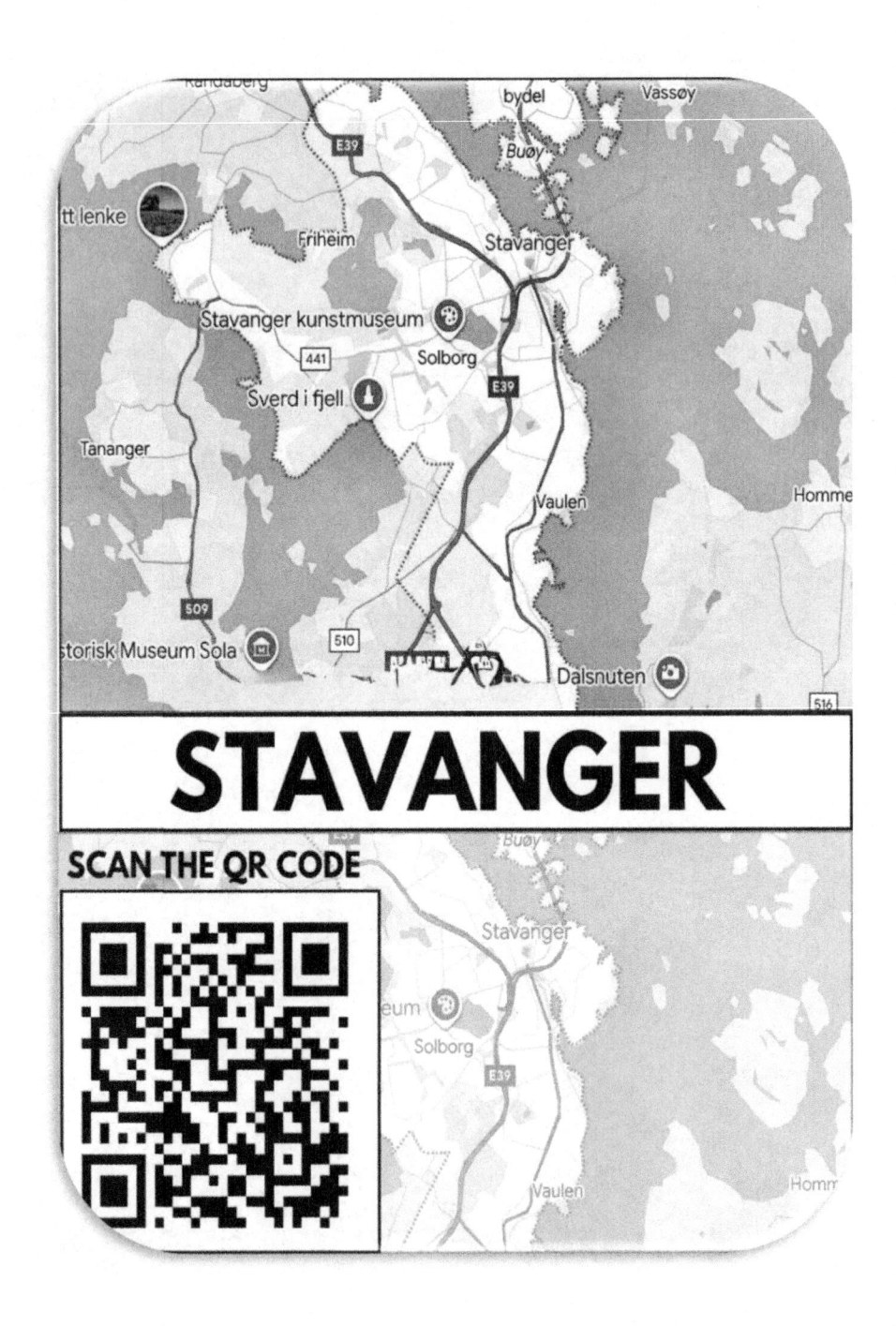

STAVANGER

SCAN THE QR CODE

Chapter 5

Adventures in the Norwegian Fjords: Outdoor Activities and Cultural Experiences

The Norwegian fjords offer a breathtaking landscape filled with adventure and cultural discoveries. Whether you're a nature enthusiast, thrill-seeker, or someone eager to immerse yourself in local traditions, this chapter covers the best ways to explore this spectacular region.

For outdoor lovers, **hiking and nature walks** take you through dramatic cliffs, lush valleys, and scenic fjordside trails. **Cycling through the fjords** offers a thrilling way to experience Norway's rugged beauty, while **kayaking and RIB boat adventures** bring you up close to towering waterfalls and serene waters. Wildlife enthusiasts can enjoy **whale watching** in the Arctic or spot **reindeer** roaming the countryside.

Beyond nature, the fjords also hold rich cultural treasures. For those seeking high-energy excursions, **glacier tours and dog sledding** provide unforgettable, adrenaline-filled experiences. This chapter guides you through the ultimate fjord adventure.

Hiking and Nature Walks

When you're cruising through the stunning Norwegian Fjords, there are plenty of ways to get out and explore the landscape in more detail. Whether you want to challenge yourself with an adventurous hike, cruise through the fjords on a kayak, or cycle through some of the most breathtaking landscapes in the world, Norway has it all.

Norway is renowned for its incredible hiking trails, offering everything from easy nature walks to more challenging mountain hikes. The Norwegian Fjords are surrounded by dramatic mountains, lush valleys, and scenic landscapes, making them a hiker's paradise.

What to Expect:

Hiking in Norway is a special experience, with well-maintained trails and unbeatable views. Whether you're hiking to a waterfall, climbing to a mountain peak, or strolling along a peaceful fjord, you'll find that the natural beauty of the Norwegian landscape takes center stage.

Popular Trails:

- **The Romsdalseggen Ridge**: One of the most popular hikes in the region, this trail offers sweeping views of **Romsdalsfjorden**, the **Trollveggen cliffs**, and surrounding mountains. The hike is challenging but offers a rewarding vista from the top.
- **The Preikestolen (Pulpit Rock)**: Although not located directly in the fjords, **Pulpit Rock** is a must-do hike if you're close to **Lysefjord**. It's one of Norway's most famous hikes, offering a thrilling view over the fjord from a dramatic cliffside.
- **Vidden Trail**: Located between **Ulrikken** and **Fløyen** in Bergen, this is a relatively moderate trail that takes you through the scenic mountain terrain with beautiful views of the city and fjords below.

Guided Tours:

While many trails are well-marked and can be done independently, taking a guided tour can enrich your experience. Guides provide interesting insights into the history, flora, and fauna of the area. Companies such as **Norway Hut to Hut**

Hiking offer guided hiking tours in various parts of Norway, ensuring you get the most out of your hike.

Contact Information for Hiking (Norway Hut to Hut Hiking):

- **Contact**: info@norwayhuttohuthiking.com | +47 22 55 60 70.
- **Website**: www.norwayhuttohuthiking.com
- **Address**: Storgata 3, 0155 Oslo, Norway.
- **Opening Hours:** Monday - Friday.

Cycling Through the Fjords

Cycling is a fantastic way to experience the fjords up close, allowing you to travel at your own pace while soaking in the natural beauty around you. Norway offers a variety of cycling routes that range from leisurely rides along coastal roads to challenging mountain paths.

What to Expect:

Cycling through the fjords is an unforgettable experience. The terrain can be hilly, but the effort is worth it when you reach a stunning viewpoint or cycle past a crystal-clear lake. You'll ride through picturesque villages, past dramatic cliffs, and alongside peaceful fjords, with opportunities to stop and explore at your leisure.

Popular Cycling Routes:

- **Geirangerfjord**: This region offers both short rides along the fjord and longer routes through the surrounding mountains. You'll cycle past small farms, traditional Norwegian houses, and enjoy breathtaking views of the fjord.
- **Lofoten Islands**: The Lofoten Islands are famous for their **dramatic peaks** and **secluded beaches**, making

them a great destination for cycling enthusiasts. The routes here offer a mix of coastal cycling and mountain challenges.

- **The Rallarvegen**: Known as one of Norway's most scenic cycling routes, **Rallarvegen** runs through the mountains and valleys, offering an amazing cycling adventure with views of waterfalls, rivers, and lush forests.

Bike Rentals and Tours:

In most of the larger fjord towns, you'll find **bike rental shops** that allow you to rent a bike for a day or longer. You can also book guided cycling tours, where a local guide will lead you along the best routes and ensure you don't miss out on any hidden gems. Companies like **Norway By Bike** offer a range of cycling tours throughout Norway, from easy coastal rides to more challenging mountain routes.

Contact Information for Cycling Tours (Norway by Bike):

- **Contact**: info@norwaybybike.com | +46 (0)8-640 96 56.
- **Website**: www.norwaybybike.com
- **Address**: Norway By Bike, 0250 Oslo, Norway.

- **Price Range:** Varies depending on the tour package and services selected. For example, the "Island Hopping Helgeland" bike tour is priced at NOK 16,500 per person in a double room.

Kayaking and RIB Boat Adventures

If you want to experience the fjords from a completely different perspective, then **kayaking** and **RIB boat adventures** are two of the most thrilling ways to explore the water. Both activities allow you to get up close to the natural beauty of the fjords, and offer an adrenaline rush in the process.

Kayaking:

Kayaking in the fjords is an incredible experience, especially when you're gliding through tranquil waters surrounded by towering cliffs. Whether you're paddling past a waterfall or exploring the **hidden coves** of a fjord, kayaking gives you a sense of intimacy with nature that's hard to beat.

What to Expect:

Guided kayaking tours are available in most major fjord towns, and they cater to all skill levels, from beginners to more experienced paddlers. You'll be provided with all the necessary gear, including waterproof suits, life vests, and paddles. Popular areas for kayaking include **Geirangerfjord**, **Sognefjord**, and **Aurlandsfjord**, where you can experience the fjords from a unique vantage point.

RIB Boat Adventures:

For those seeking a faster-paced adventure, **RIB (Rigid Inflatable Boat) boat trips** are an exciting way to explore the fjords. These high-speed boats will take you through the fjords, allowing you to see more of the area in less time. You'll get to zip across the water, spotting wildlife and admiring the dramatic landscapes from a thrilling perspective.

What to Expect:

RIB boat trips usually last 1-2 hours, and you'll be taken to some of the most spectacular parts of the fjord. Some tours also offer stops at remote islands or visits to hidden caves. You might even see seals, otters, and sea eagles along the way. **Wildlife spotting** and **water-based exploration** are the highlights of these trips.

Contact Information for Kayaking and RIB Boat Adventures:

Kayaking Tours (Nordic Ventures AS):

- **Contact**: info@nordicventures.com | +47 56 51 00 17.
- **Website**: www.nordicventures.com
- **Address**: Gudvangen, 5747 Norway.
- **Opening Hours:** Monday – Sunday: 8:00 AM - 5:00 PM.

RIB Boat Adventures (Adventure Tours):

- **Contact**: post@adventuretours.no | +47 95 76 63 85.
- **Website**: https://www.adventuretours.no/
- **Address**: Adventure Tours AS, 6876 Skjolden, Norway.
- **Opening Hours:** Monday to Sunday.

Additional Information

When to Visit:

The best time for outdoor activities in the Norwegian Fjords is during the **summer months** (June to August), when the weather is mild, and the days are long. However, **spring** and **autumn** offer fewer crowds and are great times for hiking and cycling, as the landscapes are particularly beautiful during these seasons. For **kayaking** and **RIB boat adventures**, summer is ideal, as the waters are calm and the weather is warmer.

Getting Around:

All of these activities are typically arranged through local tour operators, so you can easily book excursions from the cruise port or your hotel. For more remote areas, many tour companies provide **pickup services** from the cruise terminals or hotels.

Wildlife Watching: From Whales to Reindeer

Norway's diverse ecosystems and vast wilderness make it an ideal location for wildlife watching. From the depths of the fjords to the Arctic tundra, Norway is home to some incredible species that you can see up close on guided tours.

Whale Watching

One of the most popular wildlife experiences in Norway is **whale watching**. The waters surrounding the Norwegian coast, especially around **Tromsø** and **Andenes**, are prime feeding grounds for whales. The most commonly spotted whales include **humpback whales**, **orcas**, and **sperm whales**. These magnificent creatures migrate to the cold waters in search of fish, making this the perfect place to witness them in their natural habitat.

What to Expect:

Most whale watching tours last between 3 and 5 hours, depending on the location and type of tour. You'll head out on a boat, guided by experts who know the best spots for whale sightings. While sightings are not guaranteed, these tours increase your chances by following whale migration patterns.

Along the way, you might also spot **seals**, **dolphins**, and **sea eagles**.

Best Time to Go:

The best months for whale watching in Norway are **October through January** when the whales migrate through the fjords and surrounding waters.

Reindeer and Arctic Wildlife

Beyond the sea, Norway's **Arctic tundra** offers opportunities to see **reindeer**, **wild boar**, and **Arctic foxes**. In the northern regions, particularly near **Tromsø** and **Finnmark**, herds of **reindeer** roam freely, and you can even visit Sami reindeer herders and learn about their traditions and culture. Reindeer watching is particularly popular in **winter** when the snow-covered landscape creates a beautiful contrast with the animals.

What to Expect:

You'll typically go on a **guided safari tour** or **sleigh ride** to get a closer look at these animals in their natural environment. Many tours also include stops at Sami villages, where you can meet local people and learn about their history and traditions.

Contact Information for Wildlife Watching:

Whale Watching Tours (Arctic Whale Tours):

- **Contact**: info@arcticwhaletours.com | +47 473 84 621 (Stø), +47 48 15 10 97 (Andenes).

- **Website**: www.arcticwhaletours.com

- **Address**: Fiskeværsveien 17, 8438 Stø, Norway; Hamnegata 67 F, 8480 Andenes, Norway.

- **Reindeer and Arctic Wildlife Tours**:

- **Contact**: info@arcticwildlifetours.com | +47 95 89 77 30.

- **Website**: https://arcticwildlifetours.com/

- **Price Range**: Prices vary by tour; for example, **Golden Eagle photo hides** are NOK 2,300 per day, while Arctic expeditions start from NOK 48,500 Tromsø, Norway.

Exploring Norwegian Culture: Museums, Food, and Local Life

Norwegian culture is rich and diverse, with influences from its coastal heritage, the Sami people, and the rugged landscapes that have shaped the country's history. Exploring the culture of Norway is as much about experiencing the **history**, **art**, and **food** as it is about meeting the friendly locals.

Museums and Historical Sites

Norway is home to several fascinating museums that provide insight into the country's past. In **Oslo**, the **Viking Ship Museum** and the **Norwegian Folk Museum** offer visitors a glimpse into the ancient history of the Viking Age and rural Norwegian life. For art enthusiasts, the **National Gallery** houses iconic works by Norwegian artists like **Edvard Munch**, best known for the painting **The Scream**.

In **Bergen**, the **Bryggen Museum** is located in the heart of the UNESCO-listed **Bryggen Wharf** and explores the history of the Hanseatic merchants who once controlled trade in the region.

What to Expect:

Museums in Norway are generally interactive and educational, offering a mix of exhibitions that cater to both adults and children. Many museums offer guided tours to provide context and background on the exhibits.

Norwegian Food and Local Life

A trip to Norway wouldn't be complete without trying its delicious food. Norway is famous for its **fresh seafood**, especially **salmon** and **cod**. **Lutefisk**, a traditional dish made from dried fish, and **rakfisk**, a fermented fish delicacy, are must-tries for those looking to experience authentic Norwegian flavors. Many cities, like **Oslo** and **Bergen**, have local markets where you can taste a wide variety of foods and shop for local delicacies.

Norwegian Pastries:

Norwegians love their sweets, and **kanelbolle** (cinnamon buns) and **krumkake** (a type of waffle cookie) are beloved treats. In **Tromsø**, visit local cafés for a taste of freshly baked goods and traditional coffee.

What to Expect:

You'll find that dining in Norway is typically hearty and unpretentious. Meals often include fresh bread, cheese, and cold cuts, with many dishes focused on local, seasonal ingredients.

For a unique cultural experience, try dining in a **traditional Sami tent** (lavvu) or enjoy a meal at one of the country's fine-dining restaurants, which often serve modern interpretations of traditional Norwegian dishes.

Contact Information for Norwegian Culture:

- **Viking Ship Museum (Oslo)**:

The Viking Ship Museum in Oslo is currently closed for renovation and is scheduled to reopen in 2027 as the Museum of the Viking Age.

  o **Contact:** postmottak@khm.uio.no | +47 22 13 52 80.

  o **Website:** https://www.vikingtidsmuseet.no/

  o **Address**: Huk Aveny 35, 0287 Oslo, Norway.

  o **Opening Hours:** To be announced closer to the reopening date in 2027.

- **Bryggen Museum (Bergen)**:

  o **Contact:** bryggen@museum.no | +47 55 30 80 30.

  o **Website:** www.bymuseet.no

  o **Address**: Address: Dreggsalmenning 3, 5003 Bergen, Norway.

- **Opening Hours:** Monday – Sunday: 10:00 AM - 3:00 PM.

- **Price Range:** Adults: NOK 80–160; Students: NOK 50–80; Children 0–17 years: Free–80; BT Fordel (discount card): NOK 75–120.

- **Bergen Food Tours**:

  - **Contact**: info@bergenfoodtours.com | +47 96 04 48 92.

  - **Address**: Bryggen, 5003 Bergen, Norway.

  - **Opening Hours:** Monday – Friday: 11:00 AM - 2:00 PM.

  - **Price Range:** Approximately NOK 750 - NOK 1250 per person.

Excursions for Adventure Seekers: Glacier Tours, Dog Sledding, and More

For those seeking adrenaline-pumping activities, Norway has an abundance of adventurous excursions that will satisfy every thrill-seeker. From **glacier tours** to **dog sledding**, there's no shortage of activities to keep you excited during your visit.

Glacier Tours

Norway's glaciers are among the most accessible in the world, and there's no better way to explore them than on a guided **glacier hike**. The **Jostedalsbreen Glacier**, located in **Jostedal**, is one of the largest glaciers in Europe and offers a range of guided tours for all levels. You can also try **glacier kayaking**, where you paddle along ice-cold waters surrounded by towering glaciers.

What to Expect:

Glacier hikes are typically guided by professional guides who will provide all the necessary equipment, including **crampons**, **ice axes**, and **harnesses**. Some tours are suitable for beginners, while others require more experience. The scenery is absolutely stunning, with ice caves, crevasses, and dramatic mountain views.

Best Time to Go:

Glacier tours are best during the **summer months** (June to September), but there are **winter tours** available for those looking for a true adventure in the snow and ice.

Dog Sledding

Dog sledding in Norway is an unforgettable way to explore the Arctic wilderness. In areas like **Tromsø** and **Alta**, you can experience the thrill of driving your own dog sled or riding along with a professional musher. These tours often take you through **snow-covered landscapes**, fjords, and forests, offering a unique way to connect with nature.

What to Expect:

Most dog sledding tours last a few hours and provide all the gear you need, including **thermal suits** to keep you warm. Some tours also offer overnight trips, where you stay in **Sami-style tents** (lavvu) with your dogs, enjoying a true Arctic adventure.

Other Adventure Activities:

Glacier tours and dog sledding, Norway offers a range of other activities such as **snowmobiling**, **ice fishing**, and **skiing** in regions like **Lyngen Alps** and **Lofoten Islands**.

Contact Information for Adventure Seekers:

- **Glacier Tours**:

  o **Contact**: booking@glaciertour.no | +47 40 67 34 93.

  o **Website**: www.glaciertour.no

  o **Address**: Address: Hopsvegen 59, 6924 Hardbakke, 4636 Solund, Norway.

  o **Opening Hours:** Monday – Saturday: 07:00 AM - 6:00 PM; Sundays: 11:00 AM - 6:00 PM.

  o **Price Range:** Varies by tour; for example, the "Explore Sognefjord" tour is priced at approximately 1,950 NOK per adult.

- **Dog Sledding (Arctic Adventure Tours)**:

  o **Contact**: post@arcticadventuretours.no | +47 45 63 52 88.

  o **Website**: www.arcticadventuretours.no.

  o **Address**: Straumsvegen 993, 9109 Kvaløya, Tromsø, Norway.

  o **Opening Hours:** Monday–Friday: 08:00AM – 5:00PM.

- **Price Range:** Prices vary by activity; for example, self-drive husky dog sledding is around 4,700 NOK per person.

- **Ice Fishing (Skadi Adventures AS)**:

  - **Contact**: booking@skadi-adventures.no | +47 41 47 04 78.

  - **Website**: https://www.skadi-adventures.no/

  - **Address**: Midtre Solligarden 4, 9020, Trommsdalen, Norway.

  - **Opening Hours:** Monday – Friday: 08:00 AM - 8:00 PM; Saturday and Sundays: 10:00 AM - 4:00 PM.

  - **Price Range:** From 2,100 NOK per person.

160 | Norwegian Fjords Cruise Travel Guide 2025

Chapter 6

Norwegian Cuisine: What to Expect

Norway is known for its fresh, high-quality ingredients, and its cuisine is a reflection of the country's connection to the sea, mountains, and forests. Whether you're dining in a restaurant overlooking a stunning fjord or enjoying a meal onboard your cruise, the food on your Norwegian Fjords adventure will be a highlight. This chapter will guide you through what to expect from **Norwegian cuisine**, the **dining options onboard**, and the **specialty restaurants** that offer a taste of local delicacies.

Norwegian cuisine is deeply rooted in the country's geography, with a strong emphasis on **fresh fish, game meats**, and locally-sourced ingredients. Whether you're dining ashore or on the cruise ship, you'll find that meals are hearty, flavorful, and often simple but delicious.

Fresh Seafood:

Given Norway's long coastline, it's no surprise that seafood plays a central role in Norwegian cooking. **Salmon, cod**, and **herring** are staples, and many dishes feature fish in various forms—from smoked to pickled to fried. **Lutefisk**, dried fish reconstituted with lye, is a traditional dish often served during the Christmas season, and **Rakfisk**, fermented fish, is another delicacy you might come across during your trip.

Meat and Game:

Game meat, especially **reindeer** and **elk**, is another staple of Norwegian cuisine, with many dishes incorporating these meats in stews or roasts. For a true taste of the Arctic, you can try **reindeer steaks** or **reindeer stew**. You'll also find **lamb** in various forms, often served with potatoes and vegetables.

Traditional Norwegian Dishes:

Some traditional dishes to look out for include **Kjøttkaker** (Norwegian meatballs), **Raspeballer** (potato dumplings), and **Pølse med lompe** (Norwegian hot dogs served in a flatbread). For dessert, you might encounter **Krumkake**, a delicate Norwegian waffle cookie, or **Bløtkake**, a classic Norwegian sponge cake filled with cream and berries.

What to Expect on the Ship:

When dining onboard, you can expect to find many of these traditional Norwegian dishes, as cruise ships often focus on offering fresh, locally-inspired meals. The cuisine onboard is usually seasonal and features ingredients sourced from local markets along the Norwegian coast.

Recommended Contact Information for Norwegian Cuisine:

- **Visit Norway:**

    - **Contact:** info@visitnorway.com | +47 23 28 29 00.
    - **Website:** www.visitnorway.com
    - **Address:** Grev Wedels plass 9, 0151 Oslo, Norway
    - **Opening Hours:** Monday–Friday: 08:00AM – 4:00PM.

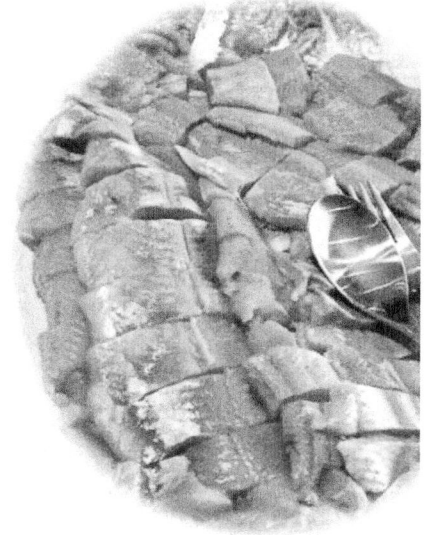

Lutefisk.   Rakfisk.

Kjøttkaker.

Raspeballer.

Pølse med lompe.

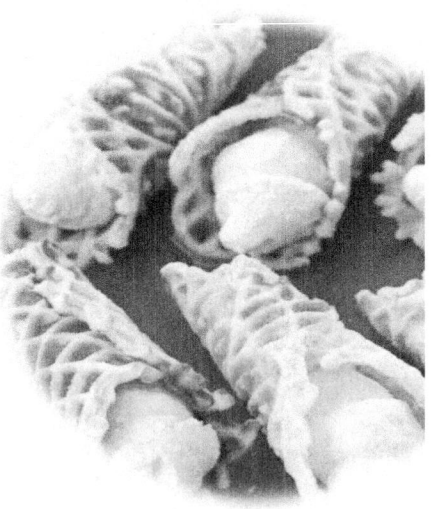

Krumkake.

Dining Options Onboard: From Buffets to Fine Dining

On your Norwegian Fjords cruise, dining options onboard will cater to a wide range of tastes, from casual buffets to elegant fine dining. Whether you're after a quick bite between excursions or a gourmet experience to mark the end of your day, there's something for everyone onboard.

Buffet Dining:

Most cruise ships offer a buffet-style dining option, where you can enjoy a wide variety of dishes at your leisure. These buffets often feature international cuisine alongside Norwegian specialties like **salmon**, **herring**, and **cheese**. Buffets are ideal for casual dining, allowing you to sample a little bit of everything or choose something you're craving. Onboard buffets also tend to be well-stocked with breakfast options, sandwiches, salads, and desserts.

Main Dining Room:

If you prefer a more traditional dining experience, the main dining room typically offers a multi-course menu with set seatings. Meals here are usually formal, with a variety of

Norwegian and international dishes served over several courses. You'll find that the main dining room is perfect for more intimate dinners and occasions.

Casual Dining:

Many cruise ships also offer **casual dining venues**, including cafés, grills, or bistros. These spots are perfect for when you want a lighter meal, like a **burger**, **pizza**, or **salad**, without the formality of the main dining room. You'll often find outdoor seating with stunning views of the fjords, especially during warm months.

Contact Information for Dining Onboard:

- **Cruise Dining Information** (e.g., Viking Ocean Cruises):
  - **Contact**: guestservices@vikingcruises.com | +1 855-338-4546.
  - **Website**: www.vikingcruises.com
  - **Address**: Viking Ocean Cruises, 5700 Canoga Avenue, Suite 200, Woodland Hills, CA 91367, USA.
  - **Price Range:** Usually included in fare.

Specialty Restaurants and Local Delicacies

For food lovers seeking a more refined or adventurous dining experience, many cruise ships offer **specialty restaurants** that feature upscale dining or regional delicacies.

Norwegian Seafood Restaurants:

Many cruise ships have specialized seafood restaurants, where you can enjoy fresh **Norwegian seafood** prepared with local flair. Dishes like **Gravlaks** (cured salmon), **Klippfisk** (salted cod), and **Smørbrød** (open-faced sandwiches with fish or meats) are common offerings in these specialty venues. These restaurants focus on using fresh, locally-sourced ingredients to highlight the natural flavors of Norwegian seafood.

Nordic-Inspired Cuisine:

For something truly unique, look for restaurants onboard that offer **Nordic-inspired** cuisine. These venues blend traditional Norwegian dishes with contemporary cooking techniques and modern flavors. Expect to see menu items like **reindeer** or **lingonberry sauce**, paired with fine wines and expertly crafted dishes. Some ships even feature **tasting menus** that provide a curated selection of dishes paired with regional wines and spirits.

Wine and Cheese Tastings:

Many cruises offer **wine pairings** and **cheese tastings** as part of their culinary offerings, showcasing Norwegian and Scandinavian cheeses such as **Brunost** (brown cheese) or **Jarlsberg**. These are often paired with wines from the region or internationally known vineyards.

Norwegian-Specific Dining Events:

For a special treat, you may find themed dining events onboard that celebrate Norwegian traditions, such as a **Norwegian smorgasbord** or a **traditional holiday dinner**, which offers multiple courses inspired by seasonal Norwegian specialties.

Contact Information for Specialty Restaurants and Local Delicacies:

- **Food Tours and Specialty Dining (Norway-specific)**:
- **Bergen Food Tours**:
  - **Contact:** info@bergenfoodtours.com | +47 96 04 48 92.
  - **Address**: Bryggen, 5003 Bergen, Norway.
  - **Opening Hours:** Monday – Friday: 11:00 AM - 2:00 PM.
  - **Price Range:** Approximately NOK 750 - NOK 1250 per person.

Gravlaks.

Klippfisk.

Smørbrød.

Brunost.

Drinks and Norwegian Spirits

Norway offers a rich selection of drinks, from refreshing local beers to world-famous spirits. Whether you're a fan of a classic cocktail, a fine wine, or you prefer to sample something uniquely Norwegian, there's plenty to try during your Norwegian Fjords cruise.

Local Beers and Brews

Norway is home to a number of craft breweries that focus on high-quality, locally produced beers. The country has a thriving beer culture, with breweries experimenting with everything from traditional lagers to innovative craft styles. The **Hansa Borg Bryggerier** in Bergen is one of the largest and most iconic breweries in Norway, offering a range of beers, including **Hansa Pilsner** and **Hansa Dark**.

What to Expect:

Most local Norwegian beers are well-balanced with a clean taste, perfect for sipping while enjoying the views of the fjords. You'll find a selection of **lagers**, **IPAs**, and **stouts** at many bars and restaurants onboard. When dining ashore, look for **local microbrews**, which are often made with ingredients sourced from the surrounding nature, like wild berries and herbs.

Norwegian Spirits

Norway is also known for its distinctive spirits, with **aquavit** (also known as **akevitt**) being the star of the show. This traditional Scandinavian spirit is typically flavored with herbs and spices such as caraway, dill, or fennel. It's usually served cold, as an aperitif or alongside meals.

What to Expect:

Aquavit is a great drink to pair with traditional Norwegian meals, like **herring**, **gravlaks** (cured salmon), or **lamb**. It's a key part of Norwegian celebrations, especially during **Christmas** or **Midsummer** festivities. You might also encounter **linje aquavit**, a special variety that's matured on ships, which imparts a unique maritime flavor to the spirit.

Another popular drink in Norway is **cider**, especially in the regions of **Hardangerfjord** and **Sognefjord**, where apples are abundant. The local ciders are often crisp and refreshing, with a mild sweetness that pairs perfectly with cheese or a light meal.

What to Expect Onboard

Cruise ships often feature a wide variety of **international wines**, **whiskies**, and **cocktails**, but they also embrace local flavors. Most Norwegian Fjords cruises offer a selection of

Norwegian beers and **aquavit** at the bars and restaurants. Look out for themed **Norwegian cocktail nights** or **local drink tastings** that allow you to sample a mix of Norway's finest beverages.

Contact Information for Drinks and Spirits:

- **Hansa Borg Breweries AS**:
  - **Contact**: info@hansaborg.no | +47 81 55 95 00.
  - **Website**: www.hansaborg.no
  - **Address**: Kokstadflaten 30, 5257 Kokstad, Norway.
  - **Opening Hours:** Monday – Friday: 08:00 AM - 4:00 PM.
  - **Price Range:** Approximately NOK 250 - NOK 750 per drink.

- **Norwegian Aquavit Producers**:
  - **Contact**: info@aquavit.no | +47 23 31 20 30.
  - **Website**: www.aquavit.no
  - **Address**: Norwegian Spirits, Oslo, Norway.

Vegan and Dietary Restrictions: What You Need to Know

For travelers with specific dietary needs, Norway and its cruise ships offer a variety of options to ensure everyone can enjoy delicious meals, regardless of their dietary restrictions. Whether you're vegan, gluten-free, or have other specific needs, you'll find that the Norwegian cuisine adapts to suit your preferences.

Vegan Cuisine in Norway

Norwegian cuisine traditionally revolves around fish, meat, and dairy, but in recent years, there's been a significant rise in plant-based eating. Many restaurants and cruise ships now offer **vegan options** that celebrate fresh vegetables, grains, and plant-based proteins.

What to Expect:

Onboard, you'll find that most ships offer a range of **vegan meals**, from soups and salads to plant-based burgers and pasta dishes. These meals often feature seasonal vegetables, locally sourced ingredients, and hearty grains like **barley** and **quinoa**. Expect to find **vegan versions** of traditional Norwegian dishes, such as **vegan smørbrød** (open-faced sandwiches), **vegan gravlaks** (cured carrot "salmon"), and plant-based versions of **kjøttkaker** (meatballs).

Norwegian Vegan-Friendly Restaurants:

While you're ashore, many Norwegian cities and towns have an increasing number of vegan-friendly restaurants. Cities like **Oslo**, **Bergen**, and **Tromsø** feature vegan-friendly cafés and eateries that offer local dishes with a plant-based twist. Look out for **vegan bakeries** and **vegetarian bistros** that serve everything from **vegan pastries** to hearty meals like **stews** and **lentil casseroles**.

Gluten-Free and Other Dietary Restrictions

Norway takes food allergies and dietary needs seriously, and you'll find that many restaurants and cruise ships offer **gluten-free**, **dairy-free**, and **nut-free** options. Many of the traditional Norwegian dishes, such as **sauces**, **stews**, and **roasted meats**, can be adapted to suit your needs. For dessert, you can expect options like **gluten-free cakes** or **dairy-free sorbets** made from local berries.

Cruise ships often have **dedicated dietary menus** where you can request special meals for any dietary restrictions, including **halal**, **kosher**, and **low-sodium** diets. It's a good idea to inform the cruise line of your dietary needs ahead of time, so they can ensure your meals are prepared with care.

What to Expect Onboard

Cruise ships are increasingly accommodating to various dietary needs, including vegan and gluten-free diets. You'll find **specialty menus** in the dining rooms, as well as on buffet tables, to ensure that there are options available for all guests. Additionally, many cruise ships offer **plant-based milk alternatives** like **almond milk**, **oat milk**, and **soy milk** for coffee, tea, and breakfast cereals.

Most cruise ships now include **vegan options** at every meal, so you won't need to worry about missing out on the experience. If you have any specific concerns, be sure to let the dining staff know in advance, and they will go out of their way to accommodate your preferences.

Contact Information for Vegan and Dietary Restrictions:

- **Norwegian Vegan-Friendly Restaurants**:
  - **Contact**: info@nordvegan.com | +47 96 91 11 67.
  - **Website**: www.nordvegan.no
  - **Address**: Kristian IVs gate 15b, 0162 Oslo, Norway.

This gives You detailed information on **Norwegian drinks**, **spirits**, and **dietary restrictions**, with separate contact information provided for each section. Whether you're exploring local spirits, sampling vegan dishes, or requesting a gluten-free meal onboard, you'll find that Norwegian Fjords cruises and the region itself offer a wide range of dining options to accommodate every need.

Chapter 7

Norwegian Culture and Traditions

Norwegian culture is shaped by its stunning natural landscape, rich history, and deep-rooted traditions. Whether it's the warm, welcoming nature of the people or the festivals that celebrate the changing seasons, Norway's culture reflects its long-standing connection to the sea, mountains, and Arctic regions. Understanding Norwegian culture can add an extra layer of meaning to your travels and help you connect with the people and places you visit.

What to Expect:

Norwegian culture is a blend of **outdoor activities, family-oriented values**, and a strong connection to the country's Viking heritage. The country's people are often described as **reserved** but **extremely friendly** once you get to know them. **Janteloven**, or the "Law of Jante," is an unspoken social code in Norway, which emphasizes humility and discourages boasting or drawing attention to oneself. This makes for a more **modest** society, where people take pride in their work and personal achievements but don't flaunt them.

Traditionally, Norway's culture is deeply tied to its **agricultural roots**, where **farming**, **fishing**, and **reindeer herding** have been central to life for centuries. These traditions are reflected in the food, festivals, and way of life in many parts of the country. **Midsummer festivals**, **Christmas celebrations**, and **national holidays** like **Norway's Constitution Day** (17th May) are significant cultural events that you might encounter during your travels.

What to Expect Onboard:

Cruise ships often embrace local culture by offering **Norwegian-themed events**, such as **folk music performances**, **traditional dance**, and cultural talks that showcase Norway's rich history and traditions. Onboard shops often sell traditional Norwegian items like **knitted wool sweaters** and **troll figurines**, giving you a chance to take a piece of Norwegian culture home with you.

Contact Information for Norwegian Culture:

- **Norwegian Culture and Traditions**:
    - **Contact:** info@visitnorway.com | +47 23 28 29 00.
    - **Website:** www.visitnorway.com
    - **Address:** Grev Wedels Plass 9, 0151 Oslo, Norway.
    - **Opening Hours:** Monday–Friday: 09:00AM – 3:00PM.

The Sami People and Their Heritage

The **Sami people** are the indigenous people of the **Nordic countries**, with a rich history that dates back thousands of years. Predominantly found in the northernmost parts of Norway, Sweden, Finland, and Russia's Kola Peninsula, the Sami culture has survived through centuries of change. Their heritage is deeply intertwined with the land, and their traditions have shaped much of the culture in northern Norway.

What to Expect:

The Sami are well-known for their **reindeer herding**, which has been central to their way of life for generations. These herders move their reindeer across vast landscapes, following traditional migration patterns. The Sami also have a rich tradition of **crafts** (including **duodji**, a form of handmade craftwork), **music** (with their distinctive **joik** chanting), and **unique clothing** (such as the brightly colored **gákti**, their traditional garments).

When visiting **Tromsø** or **Alta**, you can experience Sami culture through **guided tours** that include **reindeer sledding, cultural performances**, and the opportunity to meet Sami people in their traditional **lavvu** (tents). Learning about the Sami's sustainable relationship with nature can provide a deep and meaningful understanding of northern Norwegian life.

What to Expect Onboard:

Some cruise lines offer **Sami cultural experiences**, including live performances of **joik** music or storytelling sessions that share the history of the Sami people. These onboard activities help bring this unique culture to life for visitors who want to understand the Sami way of life, including their connection to the land and animals.

Recommended Contact Information for Sami Heritage:

- **Sami Siida AS**:
  - **Contact**: post@samisiida.no | +47 46 83 86 45.
  - **Website**: www.samisiida.no
  - **Address**: Øytunveien 4, Øvre Alta, Norway.
  - **Opening Hours:** Weekdays: 3:00 PM – 9:00 PM.
  - **Price Range:** Approximately NOK 1,295 for adults, and NOK 650 for children under 12.

The Role of the Vikings in Norwegian History

The **Vikings** played a pivotal role in shaping Norwegian history, and their legacy is still deeply felt in the country today. The Viking Age, which spanned from the **8th century to the 11th century**, marked a period of exploration, conquest, and cultural expansion that influenced much of northern Europe and beyond.

What to Expect:

The Vikings were skilled **shipbuilders**, **traders**, and **warriors**, and their longships allowed them to travel great distances, from **Iceland** and **Greenland** to **North America**. Today, the Viking legacy is still alive through **archaeological sites**, **museums**, and **festivals** that celebrate their culture.

In Oslo, the **Viking Ship Museum** has long been a must-visit for those interested in Viking history, showcasing remarkably well-preserved Viking ships and burial artifacts that offer deep insights into the lives of these seafaring explorers. The museum's collection includes iconic ships such as the **Oseberg**, **Gokstad**, and **Tune**, along with intricate grave goods that provide a glimpse into Viking craftsmanship, trade, and rituals. However, the museum is currently **closed for renovations** as it undergoes a major transformation into the new **Museum of the Viking Age**, set to reopen in **2027**. Once completed, the upgraded museum will offer an enhanced experience with modern exhibitions, interactive displays, and improved preservation of its world-renowned artifacts. Until then, visitors can explore Viking history at the **Historical Museum in Oslo**, which houses a selection of Viking-era objects from the original collection.

In **Bergen**, the **Bryggen Museum** offers valuable insights into the city's early history, including the Vikings' influence on trade and daily life in the region. While not primarily a Viking museum, it showcases archaeological finds from the Bryggen Wharf, revealing the connections between Viking-era trade networks and the later Hanseatic influence.

For a more immersive Viking experience, **Tromsø and the Lofoten Islands** offer exceptional sites where visitors can step back in time. The **Lofotr Viking Museum in Lofoten** is home to a full-scale reconstruction of a Viking chieftain's longhouse, the largest ever discovered in Norway. Here, visitors can engage in interactive exhibits, sail on a Viking ship, and participate in traditional activities like axe-throwing and archery.

In **Tromsø**, Viking history is intertwined with **Sami culture and Arctic exploration**, with museums and guided experiences that shed light on how Viking settlements adapted to the far north. These locations provide a hands-on journey into the world of the Vikings, making history come alive through detailed reconstructions and expert storytelling.

What to Expect Onboard:

Many cruise ships offer **Viking history-themed events**, such as **lectures, exhibitions**, or **special meals** that showcase Viking-inspired dishes. You can also participate in **Viking-themed entertainment** during your trip, including Viking re-enactments and the chance to learn about Viking shipbuilding, exploration, and craftsmanship.

Contact Information for Viking History:

Bryggen Museum (Bergen):

- **Contact**: bryggen@museum.no | +47 55 30 80 30.
- **Website**: www.bryggen.museum.no
- **Address**: Bryggens Museum, Dreggsalmenningen 3, 5003 Bergen, Norway.
- **Opening Hours**: Daily; 10:00am – 3:00pm.

- **Entry Fee**: Adults: 160 NOK | Seniors/Students: 120 NOK | Children (0–17): Free.

Lofotr Viking Museum (Lofoten):

- **Contact**: post@lofotr.no | +47 76 08 49 00.
- **Website**: www.lofotr.no
- **Address**: Vikingveien 539, 8360 Bøstad, Norway.
- **Opening Hours**: Tuesday –Saturday: 11:00AM – 5:00PM.
- **Entry Fee**: Adults: 160 NOK | Seniors/Students: 120 NOK | Children (0–17): Free.
- **Price Range**: Adults: 200 NOK | Seniors: 190 NOK | Students: 190 NOK | Children (6–15 yrs): 150 NOK.

Chapter 8

Modern Norway: Embracing Sustainability, Innovation, and Language

This chapter delves into Norway's commitment to **sustainability**, **innovative design**, and **technological advancements**. Norway has become a global leader in integrating **eco-friendly solutions**, from renewable energy practices to sustainable urban design, ensuring a harmonious balance with its pristine natural surroundings. The chapter also explores Norway's forward-thinking **architecture** and **design** approaches that blend modernity with environmental responsibility.

Furthermore, it provides essential **Norwegian language tips**, offering basic phrases to help travelers navigate the culture and communicate with locals. Whether you're exploring the country's sustainable achievements or preparing for a trip, this chapter equips readers with both knowledge and practical tools for an enriching experience in modern Norway.

Sustainability, Design, and Innovation

Norway is a country that blends its rich history with cutting-edge innovation. Known for its natural beauty and sustainable practices, Norway is also a leader in design and technology. From eco-friendly cities to innovative architecture and sustainable design, Norway is modernizing while staying true to its roots.

Sustainability in Norway

Norway is committed to maintaining its natural beauty while embracing sustainable practices. The country is known for its efforts in **renewable energy**, **electric vehicles**, and **eco-tourism**. As one of the leading countries in **hydropower** energy production, Norway is dedicated to creating a **carbon-neutral future**. The country also has a strong focus on **sustainable urban development**, with many cities embracing **green spaces**, **recycling programs**, and **energy-efficient building practices**.

What to Expect:

While visiting Norwegian cities like **Oslo**, **Bergen**, or **Tromsø**, you'll notice how clean and well-maintained the streets are, with extensive **public transport** networks that make it easy to travel around. Many buildings are designed with sustainability in mind, utilizing **natural materials** and **energy-saving technology**. **Electric cars** are common, with charging stations readily available, making it easy for residents and visitors alike to reduce their carbon footprint.

What You Can Do:

Norway encourages tourists to adopt eco-friendly practices during their travels. You can support sustainable tourism by choosing **eco-friendly tours** and respecting the local environment by avoiding waste and reducing energy consumption. Many cruises and excursions are now operated with **environmentally conscious practices**, ensuring your trip has a minimal impact on the fjords and local ecosystems.

Design and Innovation

Norwegian design is sleek, functional, and often inspired by the country's natural surroundings. The country has a rich tradition of **minimalist design**, with modern architecture that blends seamlessly into its beautiful landscapes. **Norwegian furniture** is world-renowned for its craftsmanship and simplicity, with brands like **HAY** and **Muuto** making waves internationally.

What to Expect:

In Norway, you'll find a beautiful mix of traditional design, modern architecture, and **innovative structures**. The **Oslo Opera House**, for instance, is an architectural marvel that blends into the landscape, allowing visitors to walk up its sloping roof to enjoy views of the fjord. The **Norwegian National Tourist Routes** feature stunning **architectural viewpoints** and visitor centers that are designed to provide a perfect blend of function and aesthetics.

Innovative Solutions:

Norway is also a leader in technological advancements. The country is at the forefront of the **smart city movement**, where urban spaces are being developed with **digital innovation** and **sustainability** in mind. For instance, **Oslo** has incorporated **smart technology** into its transportation systems, with **apps** that help manage everything from waste collection to energy use.

Contact Information for Modern Norway:

- **Innovasjon Norge**
  - **Contact:** info@innovasjonnorge.no | +47 22 00 25 00.
  - **Website:** www.innovasjonnorge.no

- **Address**: Grev Wedels plass 9, 0151 Oslo, Norway.

- **Opening Hours**: Monday – Friday: 09:00AM – 3:00PM.

- **Sustainable Tourism in Norway (Fjord Travel)**:

- **Contact**: booking@fjordtravel.no | +47 55 13 13 10.

- **Website**: www.fjordtravel.no

- **Address:** Edvard Griegs vei 3e, 5059 Bergen, Norway

- **Opening Hours:** Monday – Friday: 08:30PM –3:00PM; Saturday–Sunday: Closed.

- **Price Range:** The prices for tours typically start from 1,500 NOK.

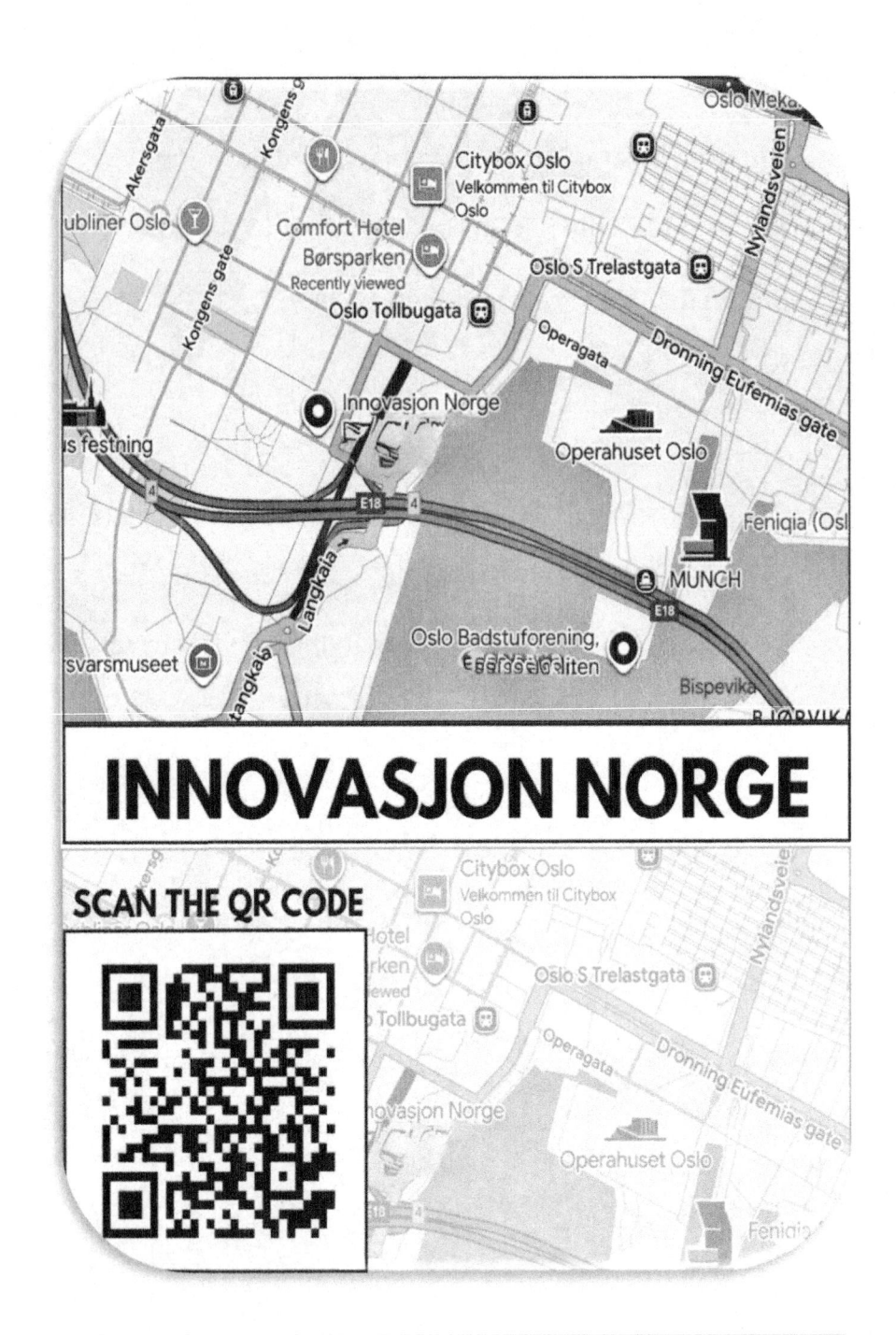

INNOVASJON NORGE

SCAN THE QR CODE

Language Tips: Basic Norwegian Phrases to Know

Norwegian is the official language of Norway, and while many people speak English fluently, learning a few basic phrases can help you connect with the locals and enrich your experience. Most Norwegians are happy to speak English, but speaking even a little Norwegian shows respect for their culture.

Basic Phrases to Know

Here are some key phrases that will help you feel more at ease while traveling through Norway. The pronunciation is straightforward, as Norwegian is a phonetic language—what you see is usually how you say it!

Greetings and Introductions

- **Hello**: *Hei* (pronounced "hi")

- **Good morning:** *God morgen* (pronounced "gooh mawr-gehn").

- **Good evening:** *God kveld* (pronounced "gooh kvel").

- **Goodnight:** *God natt* (pronounced "gooh naht").

- **Goodbye**: *Ha det* (pronounced "ha deh")

- **How are you?** - Hvordan har du det? (pronounced "vohr-dahn har doo deh?").

- **I'm fine, thank you:** Jeg har det bra, takk (pronounced "yai har deh bra, tahk").

- **What's your name?** - Hva heter du? (pronounced "hvah heh-tehr doo?")

- **My name is [name]:** Jeg heter [name] (pronounced "yai heh-tehr [name]").

Polite Phrases

- **Please**: *Vær så snill* (pronounced "vair soh snill").

- **Thank you**: *Takk* (pronounced "tahk").

- **Yes**: *Ja* (pronounced "yah").

- **No**: *Nei* (pronounced "nai").

- **Excuse me**: *Unnskyld meg* (pronounced "oohn-shild meh").

- **Sorry**: *Beklager* (pronounced "beh-klah-ger").

- **No problem:** *Ingen problem* (pronounced "een-gen proh-blehm").

- **Could you help me?** - *Kan du hjelpe meg?* (pronounced "kan doo yelp-eh mai?").

- **I don't understand**: *Jeg forstår ikke* (pronounced "yai for-stor ikh-eh")

Asking for Directions

- **Where is [place]?** - *Hvor er [place]?* (pronounced "hvor air [place]?").

- **How do I get to [place]?** - *Hvordan kommer jeg til [place]?* (pronounced "vohr-dahn koh-mehr yai teel [place]?").

- **Is it far?** - *Er det langt?* (pronounced "air deh lahngt?").

- **Turn left:** *Sving til venstre* (pronounced "sving teel vehn-streh").

- **Turn right:** *Sving til høyre* (pronounced "sving teel hoy-reh").

- **Straight ahead:** *Rett frem* (pronounced "reh-t frem").

- **Is this the right way?** - *Er dette riktig vei?* (pronounced "air deh-teh rixt-ih vehy?").

Shopping and Dining

- **Menu**: *Meny* (pronounced "meh-nee").

- **Water**: *Vann* (pronounced "vahn").

- **Coffee**: *Kaffe* (pronounced "kah-feh").

- **How much is this?** - *Hvor mye koster dette?* (pronounced "hvor meeh-eh kohs-tehr deh-teh?").

- **I would like [item], please:** *Jeg vil ha [item], vær så snill* (pronounced "yai vil hah [item], vair soh snill").

- **Do you have a menu in English?** - *Har du en meny på engelsk?* (pronounced "har doo en meh-noo poh eng-elsk?").

- **I'll have the [dish]:** *Jeg tar [dish]* (pronounced "yai tahr [dish]").

- **Water, please:** *Vann, vær så snill* (pronounced "vahn, vair soh snill").

- **Is there a vegetarian option?** - *Har dere en vegetarisk rett?* (pronounced "har deh-reh en veh-ge-tah-risk rett?").

- **I am allergic to [food]:** *Jeg er allergisk mot [food]* (pronounced "yai air ah-lehr-gisk moht [food]").

- **The food is delicious:** *Maten er deilig* (pronounced "mah-ten air day-lee").

Social Situations

- **The food is delicious:** *Maten er deilig* (pronounced "mah-ten air day-lee").

- **Nice to meet you***:* *Hyggelig å møte deg (*pronounced "hig-geh-lee oh mer-teh dai").

- **I don't speak Norwegian well:** *Jeg snakker ikke norsk godt* (pronounced "yai snah-kker eek-eh norshk goht").

- **Can you speak English?** - *Kan du snakke engelsk?* (pronounced "kan doo snahk-eh eng-elsk?").

- **I like it here:** *Jeg liker det her* (pronounced "yai lee-ker deh hair").

- **This is beautiful:** *Dette er vakkert* (pronounced "deh-teh air vahk-ert").

Common Conversation Tips

Norwegian Etiquette:

Norwegians value **politeness** and **personal space**, and greetings are typically formal. A handshake is the most common greeting. When dining or drinking, it's customary to say **"Skål"** (pronounced "skohl") before taking a sip—this means "cheers" in Norwegian.

Learn from Locals:

In many Norwegian towns, especially smaller ones, locals appreciate when visitors attempt to speak Norwegian, even if it's just a few words. Norwegians are generally understanding if you don't speak the language fluently, but they'll often offer a warm smile when you try.

Contact Information for Norwegian Language and Culture:

- **Norwegian Language Classes (Lingu Bergen)**:
  o **Contact**: lingu@lingu.no | +47 40 30 00 40.
  o **Website**: www.lingu.no
  o **Address**: Domkirkegaten 3, 5017 Bergen, Norway.
  o **Opening Hours:** Monday to Friday: 9:00 AM – 3:00 PM.

This chapter provides insights into **Modern Norway**, focusing on sustainability, design, and innovation, along with practical **language tips** and a recommended contact information to help you get around and connect with the locals.

Chapter 9

What to Buy: Traditional Handicrafts, Food, and More

Norway is a fantastic place to shop, whether you're looking for traditional handicrafts, delicious local foods, or unique fashion items. The country is known for its high-quality products, sustainability, and dedication to craftsmanship. This chapter will guide you through what to buy, where to find it, and the best shopping districts and souvenir shops in Norway.

Norwegian souvenirs are more than just trinkets. Many items reflect the country's rich cultural heritage, and they make meaningful mementos of your trip. From traditional **handicrafts** to **local foods**, here are some of the most popular things to buy while in Norway.

Traditional Handicrafts

Norway is famous for its craftsmanship, and you'll find a wide variety of **handmade goods** that make perfect souvenirs. **Knitted wool sweaters**, particularly the **Lusekofte** or **Setesdal sweater**, are iconic items that showcase traditional Norwegian knitting patterns. These sweaters are perfect for keeping warm in colder climates and are often made from **wool sourced from Norwegian sheep**.

- **Other Handicrafts**:

  o **Sami crafts** such as **duodji** (handmade tools, jewelry, and other objects) make for authentic and unique souvenirs.

  o **Wooden items** like **hand-carved troll figures, bowl spoons**, and **pillowcases** often feature Norwegian folklore and traditions.

  o **Norwegian porcelain**, particularly pieces from **Figgjo** and **Porsgrund**, is highly prized for its craftsmanship and design.

Norwegian Food and Drink

Norwegian food products make excellent gifts, especially for foodies looking to bring home a taste of the country. **Norwegian cheeses**, such as **brunost** (brown cheese) and **jarlsberg**, are delicious and uniquely Norwegian. Another popular item is **koldtbord** (a platter of cold cuts), which includes various meats, cheeses, and pickled fish, a staple of Norwegian dining.

- **Seafood and Dried Fish**:

You can bring home **dried fish** or **klippfisk** (salted cod), both of which are deeply embedded in Norwegian culinary traditions.

- **Norwegian Spirits**:

    Aquavit, the famous Norwegian spirit made from grains and flavored with caraway, dill, or fennel, is a must-try and makes an excellent souvenir.

Local Design and Fashion

Norway is also known for its **minimalist design** and modern fashion. Many designers showcase clean lines, simple shapes, and functionality in their work. You'll find **clothing** from Norwegian designers, such as **Holzweiler**, which offers stylish outerwear and accessories, and **Norwegian rain**, known for its functional yet fashionable waterproof clothing.

What to Expect:

Norwegian shopping is often centered around **sustainability**, with many brands offering eco-friendly fashion and accessories. Look for locally-made **bags**, **scarves**, and **hats**, which combine modern designs with traditional elements.

Contact Information for Norwegian Handicrafts and Products:

- **Traditional Norwegian Craftmanship (Husfliden Bergen AS)**:
    - **Contact:** bergen@norskflid.no | +47 55 54 47 40.

- Website: www.norskflid.no
- Address: Vågsallmenningen 3, 5014 Bergen, Norway.
- Opening Hours: Monday to Saturday: 9:00 AM – 5:00 PM.
- Price Range: Varies; typically between NOK 200 and NOK 5,000, depending on the product.

- **Norwegian Handicrafts (Hjertholm)**:
  - Contact: hjertholmbergen@hjertholm.no | +47 90 40 25 90.
  - Website: www.hjertholm.no
  - Address: Torgallmenningen 8, Galleriet 5. etg, 5014 Bergen, Norway.
  - Opening Hours: Monday to Saturday: 9:00 AM – 9:00 PM.

Best Shopping Districts and Souvenir Shops

Whether you're looking for high-end designer items or unique local souvenirs, Norway has plenty of great shopping districts to explore. From **Oslo** to **Bergen** to **Tromsø**, here are some of the best places to shop for Norwegian products:

Oslo: The Capital's Shopping Scene

Oslo's shopping scene offers something for every type of shopper, from high-end luxury boutiques to unique local markets, and everything in between. The city seamlessly blends modern retail with traditional Norwegian craftsmanship, making it a must-visit destination for those wanting to experience a fusion of contemporary and classic designs.

The heart of Oslo's shopping scene is **Karl Johans gate**, the city's main shopping street. Lined with an eclectic mix of stores, this bustling street is home to both international luxury brands and high-quality Norwegian-made products. For those seeking **luxury fashion**, Karl Johans gate is the place to find exclusive boutiques offering the latest trends from renowned designers. You can shop for everything from **traditional Norwegian wool garments** to cutting-edge **contemporary clothing**.

If you're looking for something uniquely Norwegian, the street also offers shops selling **Norwegian-made jewellery**, beautifully crafted wooden items, and intricate **traditional crafts**, such as **knitted scarves** and **handmade leather goods**.

Beyond Karl Johans gate, Oslo also boasts modern shopping malls such as **Oslo City** and **Aker Brygge**, which are home to a diverse range of stores, from high-street fashion brands to art galleries and lifestyle shops. For those interested in unique, locally designed items, make sure to visit the **Mathallen Food Hall** or the **Grønland district** where you'll find local markets and stores offering **artisan goods**, handmade jewellery, and **scents of Norway**.

Whether you're in the mood for luxury, handmade treasures, or contemporary fashion, Oslo's shopping scene offers a perfect blend of old and new that truly reflects the capital's dynamic culture.

- **Aker Brygge and Tjuvholmen**:

These waterfront areas are perfect for a day of shopping and dining. In addition to local shops, you'll find art galleries and design shops selling unique, Norwegian-made items. Aker Brygge is also home to several **design-focused** shops selling **modern furniture, artwork, and handmade goods**.

Norwegian Design Shops:

- **Fjordbutikken** in Oslo offers **quality handicrafts**, including **knitted wool products**, **jewelry**, and **home decor** items.

    o **Contact:** info@fjordbutikken.no | +45 30 23 96 00.

    o **Website:** https://www.fjordbutikken.dk/

    o **Address**: Ved Skoven, 8541 Skødstrup, Denmark.

Bergen: The City of Shops

Bergen's streets, particularly in the historic **Bryggen district**, are filled with quaint boutiques and artisan shops that reflect the city's rich cultural heritage. As you wander through these narrow, cobbled lanes, you'll find a delightful mix of locally crafted goods, from **Sami handicrafts** to intricately carved wooden **troll figurines**. The **Bryggen district**, a UNESCO World Heritage site, is home to small craft shops, art galleries, and unique souvenir stores offering everything from traditional Norwegian knitwear to locally produced jewelry. These shops not only showcase the region's artistic talents but also offer a chance to take home a piece of Bergen's cultural and artistic legacy. Whether you're looking for an authentic Norwegian keepsake or simply enjoying the historic surroundings, Bergen's boutique shopping scene is sure to impress.

- **What to Buy in Bergen**:

Bergen is known for its **wooden handicrafts**, so be sure to visit shops like **Bergen Husflid** for locally made **textiles**, **wooden spoons**, and **traditional Norwegian sweaters**.

- o **Contact**: bergenhus@husflid.no | +47 55 32 88 03.
- o **Website**: https://www.sweaterspecialist.com/
- o **Address**: Bryggen 19, 5003 Bergen, Norway.
- o **Opening Hours:** Monday to Friday: 09:30AM– 6:30PM; Sundays: 10:00AM–6PM.

Tromsø: Arctic Souvenirs

Tromsø, located above the Arctic Circle, is a treasure trove of unique Arctic-themed souvenirs that reflect its northern heritage and polar history. Visitors can find a variety of **reindeer skins** and **fur products**, which are not only beautiful but also practical for cold climates. Many shops in the city specialize in **Sami handicrafts**, offering handmade items like **woven baskets, traditional clothing**, and **jewelry** crafted by the indigenous Sami people. These items carry deep cultural significance, often symbolizing the rich traditions and heritage of the region. Tromsø's connection to Arctic expeditions is also evident in the range of **historical artifacts** and **polar-themed souvenirs**, from vintage maps to models of early Arctic ships. These shops offer an authentic glimpse into the fascinating history of the Arctic, making Tromsø the perfect destination for unique and meaningful keepsakes.

What to Expect:

Many souvenir shops in Tromsø offer **local handicrafts** as well as **polar bear figurines, snow globes,** and **Arctic-themed jewellery**. It is recommended that you visit **Polaria**, a center dedicated to Arctic wildlife, for more unique gifts like **Arctic-inspired art** and **scientific books** about the region.

- **Contact**: booking@polaria.no | +47 77 75 01 00.
- **Website**: www.polaria.no
- **Address**: Hjalmar Johansens gate 12, 9007 Tromsø, Norway.
- **Opening Hours**: Daily; 10:00AM– 4:00PM.

This highlights some of the best **shopping districts** and **souvenir shops** in Norway, offering insights into what you can buy, from **traditional handicrafts** to **local food** and unique **fashion items** on your trip.

Local Markets and Artisans

One of the most authentic ways to experience Norwegian culture is by visiting its local markets and meeting the artisans who create beautiful, handmade goods. These markets offer a glimpse into the traditional crafts, local food, and artistic expressions that have been passed down through generations. Whether you're looking for a unique souvenir or simply want to explore, Norwegian markets are a must-see for any traveler.

What to Expect at Local Markets

Norway's markets are filled with a variety of products that reflect the country's rich cultural heritage. From bustling street markets in Oslo to small village markets in the fjords, there's always something special waiting for you.

Crafts and Handmade Goods:

Local artisans showcase their skills in everything from **woodwork** to **ceramics, knitted textiles**, and **reindeer-skin products**. In cities like **Oslo, Bergen,** and **Tromsø**, you'll find markets where these craftsmen display their work, offering a chance to purchase authentic, locally made items like **hand-carved wooden spoons, Sami jewelry,** and **traditional wool** sweaters. These goods not only make great souvenirs but also serve as a wonderful way to support the local community.

Local Food:

Markets in Norway are also perfect for food lovers. You can taste **Norwegian cheeses**, **cured meats**, and **fresh seafood** right from the source. During the summer months, many towns host **farmers' markets** where you can buy fresh **berries**, **root vegetables**, and **herbs**. Some markets also offer **baked goods**, including **Norwegian rye bread** and **krumkake** (a traditional Norwegian pastry), all made with locally sourced ingredients.

Where to Find the Best Markets and Artisans

Oslo:

In the heart of Oslo, **Mathallen Food Hall** offers an amazing selection of local food vendors, featuring everything from traditional Norwegian pastries to fresh fish and cheeses. For handmade goods, **The Norwegian Crafts Center** is a wonderful place to find authentic pieces made by skilled artisans.

- **Contact**: post@mathallen.no | +47 40 00 12 09.
- **Website**: https://mathallenoslo.no/
- **Address**: Vulkan 5, 0178 Oslo, Norway.

- **Opening Hours:** Tuesday to Saturday: 10:00AM – 8:00PM; Sundays: 11:00AM–6PM; Monday: Closed.
- **Price Range:** Varies by vendor; generally, around 100 – 400 NOK per person.

Bergen:

The **Bergen Fish Market** is famous for its fresh seafood and is an excellent place to sample local Norwegian fish dishes. For handmade crafts, head to **Bryggen** where you can explore small artisan shops selling woodwork, textiles, and other traditional Norwegian crafts.

- **Contact**: info@bergenfisketorget.no | +47 55 55 20 00.
- **Website**: https://www.bergen.kommune.no/
- **Address**: Torget 5, 5014 Bergen, Norway.
- **Opening Hours:** Monday–Thursday: 10:00AM–9:00PM | Friday and Saturday: 10:00AM–11:00PM | Sunday: 12:00 – 9:00PM.

Tromsø:

Tromsø offers a unique market experience with its **Arctic-**

themed crafts. It is recommended that you visit the **Tromsø Christmas Market** (held during winter) or explore local shops where artisans sell **Sami-inspired products**, like **reindeer leather goods, fur items**, and handmade **jewelry**.

Supporting Local Artisans

Norway's artisans are proud of their craft, and purchasing directly from them not only supports local artists but also helps preserve traditional skills. Many markets and craft fairs feature live demonstrations, where you can watch artisans at work and learn about their techniques. Whether you're looking for a handwoven wool blanket or a hand-carved wooden bowl, buying from these markets is a way to bring a piece of Norway's rich heritage home with you.

What You'll Find:

In addition to the typical souvenirs, look for one-of-a-kind pieces such as hand-forged knives, leather goods, felt hats, and Sami drums. The quality of these items reflects the care and expertise of the artisans, many of whom use locally sourced materials such as reindeer antlers, birch wood, and Norwegian wool.

Tips for Visiting Markets:

Timing:

Local markets in Norway often operate seasonally, especially farmers' markets. The best time to visit for fresh food markets is during the **spring and summer months**. If you're looking for winter crafts or **Christmas markets**, plan your trip for **November to December**.

Cash and Payment:

While most places accept **credit cards**, it's always a good idea to carry **some cash** (Norwegian **kroner** or **NOK**) when visiting local markets, as some artisans prefer cash transactions.

This section on **Local Markets and Artisans** provides detailed insight into where to find unique and traditional Norwegian products, from handmade crafts to local food. Whether you're exploring markets in **Oslo**, **Bergen**, or **Tromsø**, you'll be able to support local artisans and take-home meaningful souvenirs.

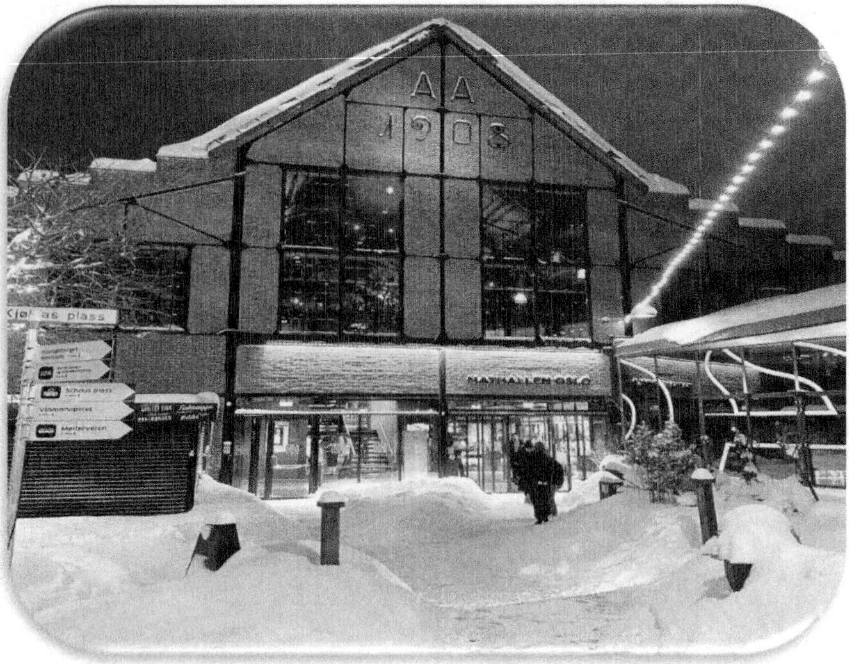
AA
1908
MATHALLEN OSLO

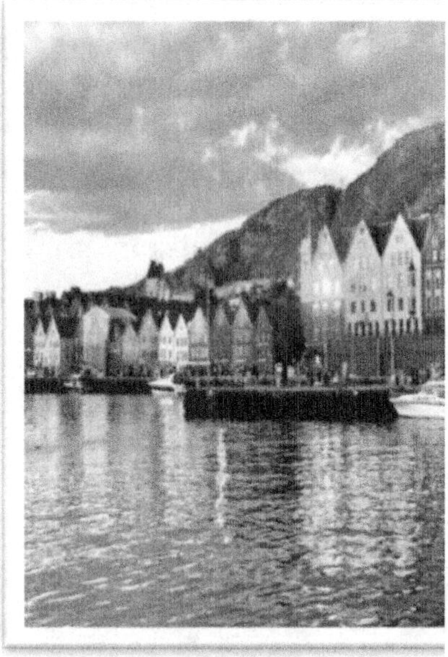

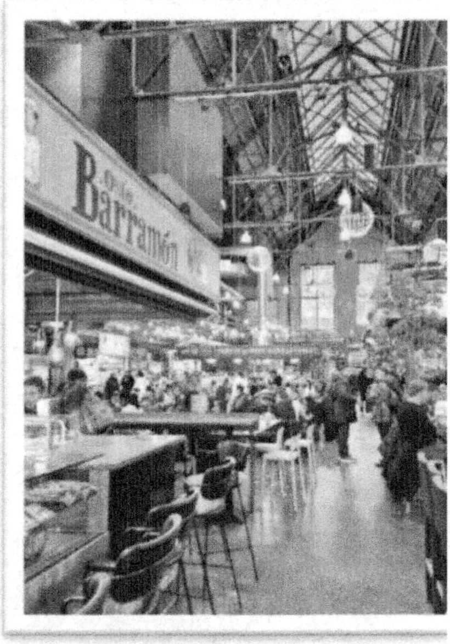
Barramón

Chapter 10

Weather in the Fjords: What to Expect Throughout the Year

When planning your trip to the Norwegian Fjords, understanding the weather is essential for making the most of your experience. The fjords are stunning year-round, but the weather can vary significantly depending on the season. Whether you're visiting during the long summer days or the dark winter months, it's important to know what to expect.

Winter (December to February)

Winter in the Norwegian Fjords is a magical time, especially for those interested in **Northern Lights** viewing. However, it's also the coldest season, with temperatures often dropping below freezing, especially in the **northern fjords**. Snowfall is common, and the landscapes are covered in a beautiful blanket of white.

What to Expect:

Daylight hours are shorter in winter, especially in the far north where the **polar night** occurs, meaning there is little to no sunlight for several weeks. The temperatures can range from **-5°C to -15°C** (23°F to 5°F) in the fjord regions, though it can feel colder with the wind chill. This is also the time of year when many outdoor activities, like **dog sledding**, **snowmobiling**, and **Northern Lights tours**, are most popular.

Spring (March to May)

Spring in the Norwegian Fjords is a time of transition. The snow begins to melt, and the landscape starts to bloom with wildflowers and greenery. Temperatures rise slowly, and while it's still chilly early in the season, it becomes much milder towards May.

What to Expect:

In March and April, you may still experience some cold weather, with temperatures ranging from **-2°C to 10°C** (28°F to 50°F). However, by May, the weather can be quite pleasant, and temperatures can reach around **10°C to 15°C** (50°F to 59°F). This is also the best time to see **waterfalls** at their most powerful, as melting snow feeds the rivers and streams.

Summer (June to August)

Summer in the fjords is short but spectacular. With the **Midnight Sun** in the north, the days stretch on for nearly 24 hours, providing plenty of time for exploration and adventure. Summer is the peak tourist season, and the fjords are alive with activities.

What to Expect:

Daytime temperatures are generally mild, ranging from **15°C to 25°C** (59°F to 77°F), though coastal areas can feel warmer, especially on sunny days. This is the best time for hiking, cruising, and outdoor adventures, with long days and relatively calm weather. The northern regions, like **Tromsø**, will still experience 24 hours of daylight, which is a surreal experience for many travelers.

Autumn (September to November)

Autumn is another stunning time to visit, with the foliage changing to vibrant reds and golds. While the weather can start to cool, it's still relatively mild compared to winter. Autumn is also the time when the **Northern Lights** start to become visible again as the nights grow longer.

What to Expect:

Temperatures in the early autumn months (September and October) range from **10°C to 15°C** (50°F to 59°F), while

November sees cooler temperatures between **5°C to 10°C** (41°F to 50°F). It's a quieter season to visit, so you can enjoy the beauty of the fjords without the crowds. Some outdoor activities like **hiking** are still possible, though it's important to be prepared for rain and wind.

What to Expect for the Weather Year-Round

Regardless of the season, the weather in the Norwegian Fjords can be unpredictable. You might experience rain or sunshine on the same day, especially in coastal areas. It's always a good idea to check the forecast ahead of time and pack for a variety of conditions, as weather patterns can change quickly in this region.

Contact Information for Weather in the Fjords:

- **Norwegian Weather Service (MET Norway)**:
    - **Contact**: post@met.no | +47 22 96 30 00.
    - **Website**: www.met.no
    - **Address**: Henrik Mohns plass 1, PO Box 43 Blindern, 0313 Oslo.
    - **Opening Hours:** Monday to Friday, 8:00 AM – 4:00 PM.

Packing for All Seasons: Layering and Waterproof Gear

Packing for your trip to the Norwegian Fjords is all about being prepared for the varying weather conditions, regardless of the time of year. While the fjords are beautiful year-round, the weather can change quickly, so it's essential to bring the right gear. **Layering** is key, and waterproof clothing is a must for all seasons.

Layering Your Clothing

Layering is the best way to ensure comfort no matter what the weather throws at you. It allows you to adjust your clothing based on the temperature and activity level.

Base Layer:

Start with a **moisture-wicking base layer** to keep sweat off your skin. Look for **thermal tops** and **bottoms** made from **merino wool** or **synthetic materials**, as they are lightweight and effective at keeping you warm without overheating.

Mid Layer:

For warmth, choose a **fleece jacket** or **down vest**. These layers will trap your body heat, which is especially important during the colder months. A **softshell jacket** is also a good option for the milder spring and autumn temperatures.

Outer Layer:

A **waterproof and windproof jacket** is essential for all seasons. The weather in the Norwegian Fjords can be unpredictable, with rain and wind being common even in summer. A **rain jacket** or **waterproof shell** will help keep you dry and comfortable while allowing for airflow to prevent you from overheating.

Footwear:

Waterproof, comfortable hiking boots are a must if you plan to explore the fjords' outdoor trails. Look for boots that are both waterproof and breathable, as well as having a good grip for slippery conditions.

Accessories:

Bring a **warm hat** and **gloves** if you're visiting in the colder months, as well as a **scarf** or **neck gaiter** to protect your face from wind and cold. In the summer, a **sun hat** is useful, especially if you're hiking in the north where the sun doesn't set.

Waterproof Gear

Regardless of the season, waterproof gear is important. This includes **waterproof jackets**, **pants**, and **backpacks**. The fjords are known for their **rain showers**, and you'll want to stay dry while enjoying the stunning scenery. For those who plan on **kayaking** or **cruising**, **waterproof bags** and **dry bags** are great for protecting your gear from getting wet.

What Else to Pack

- **Sunglasses**: Even in winter, the reflection of the snow can make it bright, so bring **polarized sunglasses** to protect your eyes.

- **Camera**: The scenery in Norway is breathtaking, so don't forget a **good camera** to capture the views.

- **Power Bank**: With long days in summer or the potential to be outdoors for hours, make sure you have a **portable charger** for your devices.

Recommended Contact Information for Packing Tips:

- **Norwegian Tourist Information**:

    - **Contact:** info@visitnorway.com | +47 23 28 29 00.
    - **Website:** www.visitnorway.com
    - **Address:** Grev Wedels Plass 9, 0151 Oslo, Norway.

Travel Essentials

Chapter 11

The Midnight Sun: Experiencing the Polar Day

One of the most remarkable natural phenomena in Norway is the **Midnight Sun**—a period when the sun doesn't set for several weeks in the far north. This experience is only possible in areas above the Arctic Circle, such as **Tromsø**, **Lofoten Islands**, and **Svalbard**, where you can witness continuous daylight, even at midnight.

What to Expect

The Midnight Sun occurs in the **summer months**, from about **mid-May to late July**, when the Earth's tilt allows the sun to remain above the horizon for 24 hours a day. During this period, you'll find that time seems to lose all meaning. **Day and night blur together**, with the sky painted in soft shades of **gold**, **pink**, and **purple**, creating a surreal, dream-like atmosphere.

Activities:

The extended daylight hours offer plenty of time for exploration. You can enjoy activities such as **hiking, kayaking, sightseeing**, or even **midnight golfing**—a unique experience in the polar day. Many visitors find that the best way to take advantage of the Midnight Sun is by going on **boat trips** or **scenic drives**, where you can enjoy the stunning landscapes without worrying about the time.

Photographing the Midnight Sun:

The soft light during the Midnight Sun provides perfect conditions for photography, especially for capturing the dramatic landscapes of Norway. The sun's low position creates long shadows, enhancing the textures of the mountains, fjords, and villages.

Where to See the Midnight Sun

- **Tromsø**: Tromsø is often called the "Gateway to the Arctic", and it's one of the best places to experience the Midnight Sun. The city is located above the Arctic Circle, and from **mid-May to late July**, you can enjoy several weeks of continuous daylight.
- **Lofoten Islands**: The **Lofoten Islands** are another excellent destination for the Midnight Sun. The islands are renowned for their dramatic scenery, with steep mountains rising from the sea. You can take a boat tour, hike to a mountain peak, or simply relax and enjoy the views.

- **Svalbard**: For the ultimate Midnight Sun experience, visit **Svalbard**, a remote archipelago located far above the Arctic Circle. Here, you'll experience nearly **four months of continuous daylight** from April to August, with no true nightfall.

Contact Information for the Midnight Sun Experience:

Tromsø Tourism:

- **Contact:** info@visittromso.no | +47 77 61 00 00.
- **Website**: www.visittromso.no
- **Address**: Storgata 83, Postbox 311, 9253 Tromsø, Norway.
- **Opening Hours:** Monday–Friday: 09:00AM–5:00PM | Saturday: 09:00AM–4:00PM | Sunday: 10:00AM–3:00PM.

Lofoten Islands:

- **Contact:** info@lofoten.no | +47 76 09 50 00.
- **Website:** https://visitlofoten.com/en/
- **Address**: Lofoten Tourist Information, 8300 Svolvær, Norway.
- **Opening Hours:** Monday to Friday 9:00 AM to 5:00 PM.

Northern Lights: When and Where to See Them

The **Northern Lights**, or **Aurora Borealis**, are one of nature's most spectacular shows, and Norway offers some of the best opportunities to witness this incredible phenomenon. The swirling colors of green, purple, and pink dance across the Arctic sky, creating an unforgettable display.

When to See the Northern Lights

The best time to see the Northern Lights in Norway is during the **winter months**, from **late September to early April**, with the peak season being between **October and March**. During this period, the nights are longest and darkest, providing optimal conditions for Northern Lights viewing. The lights are most visible on **clear, crisp nights** away from artificial light pollution.

What to Expect:

While you can't predict exactly when the Northern Lights will appear, you can increase your chances by heading to areas above the Arctic Circle, where the aurora is most commonly seen. The lights are best viewed during the **night**—the darker, the better. Northern Lights can appear as a faint glow or a bright display of waves and arcs moving across the sky.

Where to See the Northern Lights

Tromsø

Tromsø, renowned as one of the best destinations to witness the Northern Lights, offers a wide range of guided tours that take you deep into the Arctic wilderness for optimal viewing. Experienced guides lead excursions through pristine snow-covered landscapes, enhancing your chances of seeing the **Aurora Borealis**. Popular options include **dog sledding**, where you can glide through frozen terrain, and **snowshoeing**, offering a more intimate way to explore the region's beauty. Additionally, **Northern Lights cruises** provide a stunning vantage point from the water, allowing you to chase the lights along the fjords. Each tour is carefully designed to maximize your experience, offering both the thrill of adventure and the magic of this natural spectacle in one of the world's most remote locations.

Alta

Alta, often known as the "City of the Northern Lights", is a **must-visit destination** for those eager to witness the aurora borealis in its full glory. Nestled in **Finnmark**, the northernmost county in **Norway**, Alta offers **some of the darkest skies** in the country, making it an ideal location for **aurora hunting**. From **late September to early April**, the city enjoys clear, dark nights, far from the light pollution of larger cities, ensuring a **spectacular, vivid view** of the Northern Lights.

A standout attraction in Alta is the **Northern Lights Cathedral**, a striking **architectural marvel** that beautifully reflects the natural beauty of the aurora. Designed with elements that echo the northern landscapes, the cathedral offers a spiritual and visual experience that enhances the city's northern lights appeal. Alta's remote location and clear skies create a truly magical atmosphere, making it an exceptional spot to experience this incredible natural phenomenon. It's truly a magical place for northern lights lovers.

Svalbard

Svalbard offers one of the most unique Northern Lights experiences, set within the Arctic wilderness. Unlike other destinations, Svalbard's **polar night** lasts from **mid-November to late January**, offering nearly 24 hours of darkness, which creates the perfect conditions for witnessing the **Aurora Borealis**. The tour takes you through remote landscapes, including **glaciers, fjords,** and **mountain ranges**, providing an intimate and serene backdrop to the lights. Many tours are conducted by **local guides** who are experts in Arctic weather patterns and provide insight into the science behind the aurora. What sets Svalbard apart is its isolation; there's little light pollution, and you often find yourself in an **untouched environment**, far from the crowds. The chance to witness the Northern Lights here, amidst such raw natural beauty, is truly a once-in-a-lifetime experience.

Contact Information for Northern Lights Viewing:

- **Tromsø Northern Lights Tours**:
  - **Contact**: info@chasinglights.com | +47 92 29 15 55.
  - **Website**: www.chasinglights.com
  - **Address**: Storgata 64A, 9008 Tromsø, Norway.
  - **Opening Hours:** Monday–Friday: 09:00AM–6:00PM; Saturday: 10:00AM–4:00PM; Sunday: Closed.

- **Alta Northern Lights Tours (Luoso AS Northern Lights Tours)**:
  - **Contact**: info@luuso.no | +47 78 44 00 00.
  - **Website**: www.luuso.no

- **Address**: Markedsveien 1, 9510 Alta, Norway.

- **Opening Hours:** Monday to Friday: 9:00AM – 5 PM.

• **Svalbard Northern Lights Tours (Basecamp Explorer Spitsbergen):**

- **Contact**: spitsbergen@basecampexplorer.com | +47 79 02 46 00.

- **Website**: www.basecampexplorer.com

- **Address**: Vei 223, 6, 9171 Longyearbyen, Svalbard, Norway.

- **Opening Hours:** Monday–Friday: 9:00AM–5PM; Saturday: 10:00 AM–4PM; Sunday: Closed.

229 | Norwegian Fjords Cruise Travel Guide 2025

230 | Norwegian Fjords Cruise Travel Guide 2025

Chapter 12

Staying Healthy Onboard: Facilities and Services

While cruising through the stunning Norwegian fjords, it's important to keep your health in mind. Fortunately, most cruise ships offer excellent onboard facilities and services designed to ensure your well-being throughout the journey.

What to Expect Onboard

Cruise ships are well-equipped with modern health facilities, including **fitness centers**, **spas**, and **wellness programs** to keep you feeling your best. Many ships offer a variety of **yoga classes**, **Pilates**, and **aerobics**, perfect for stretching and staying active during your time at sea. If you're in need of relaxation, the **spa** offers everything from **massages** to **sauna sessions**, ensuring you unwind after a day of exploration.

Onboard Medical Services

Every cruise ship has a **medical center**, staffed with trained professionals who can help in case of minor health issues. This facility provides basic medical care, including **over-the-counter medications**, first aid, and consultations for common ailments. For more serious medical needs, larger ships are equipped with **telemedicine services**, which allow remote consultations with medical professionals on land.

Medical Insurance:

Before boarding, it's essential to ensure you have adequate **travel insurance** that covers medical emergencies. It's always a good idea to check with your cruise provider about their onboard medical services, especially if you have specific health needs.

Emergency Procedures:

Cruise lines have established **emergency medical protocols** for serious medical incidents, including access to nearby hospitals in port and the ability to transport patients to land-based facilities if necessary. In case of severe emergencies, the ship is equipped with **evacuation procedures** to ensure passenger safety.

Contact Information for Onboard Health Services:

- **Cruise Ship Medical Services (e.g., Viking Ocean Cruises)**:
  - **Contact**: health@vikingcruises.com | +1 855-818-4546.
  - **Website**: www.vikingcruises.com

- **Address**: Viking Ocean Cruises, 5700 Canoga Avenue, Suite 200, Woodland Hills, CA 91367, USA.

Medical Emergencies and Cruise Ship Protocols

It's always a good idea to prepare for the possibility of medical emergencies while traveling, especially on a cruise. Fortunately, cruise ships have clear protocols in place to deal with various situations and ensure passengers receive the care they need quickly and efficiently.

Medical Emergencies Onboard

Most cruise ships are equipped with an **onboard doctor** and **nurses** who can handle anything from minor injuries to more serious health problems. In case of an emergency, the ship's crew will assist with getting you medical help promptly, either onboard or by coordinating with local emergency services at port.

Cruise Ship Medical Protocols:

Cruise ships have comprehensive **first aid kits** and medical equipment available. If a medical situation arises that cannot be treated onboard, the ship will often **coordinate with local hospitals** or **arrange medical evacuation** to the nearest healthcare facility if needed. It's important to notify the crew immediately if you feel unwell so they can activate the necessary protocols.

Emergency Contacts:

In the event of a medical emergency, the cruise staff can provide assistance in contacting your **insurance provider** or **family members**. Ensure that you carry an **emergency contact card** with you, including your **insurance details** and important health information.

What You Should Do in an Emergency:

- Stay calm and contact the ship's medical center immediately.

- Follow the ship's protocols and instructions from the onboard medical team.

- Have a list of any pre-existing conditions, medications, or allergies readily available for medical staff.

Contact Information for Cruise Ship Medical Emergencies:

- **Cruise Ship Emergency Support (e.g., Royal Caribbean)**:

  o **Contact**: info@rccl.com | +1 800-256-9619.

  o **Website**: www.royalcaribbean.com

  o **Address**: Royal Caribbean Cruises Ltd., 1050 Caribbean Way, Miami, FL 33132, USA.

Avoiding Seasickness and Travel Illnesses

Seasickness and other travel-related illnesses are common concerns for many cruise passengers, but there are ways to prevent or manage these conditions. Being proactive about your health can ensure you enjoy the stunning landscapes and activities without discomfort.

Preventing and Managing Seasickness

Seasickness is typically caused by the motion of the ship, which can affect your inner ear and sense of balance. If you're prone to seasickness, it's important to take preventative measures, especially when the ship is in open waters or during rough weather.

Before Your Cruise:

If you're worried about seasickness, consider **taking anti-nausea medication** before your trip. Over-the-counter remedies like **Dramamine** or **Bonine** can be effective. Some passengers find **acupressure wristbands** helpful, which work by applying pressure to a point on your wrist that can help control nausea.

While Onboard:

- Choose a **midship cabin** on lower decks, as these areas experience less motion.

- Spend time on **deck** where the fresh air and horizon will help keep your equilibrium balanced.

- **Eat light meals** and avoid greasy or spicy foods, which can trigger nausea.

- **Hydrate**:
  Drinking plenty of **water** and staying hydrated can also help prevent seasickness. Avoid **alcohol** and **caffeinated drinks**, as they can exacerbate symptoms.

Other Travel Illnesses

Cruise ships can sometimes be crowded, and illness can spread quickly in confined spaces. Here are some simple tips to stay healthy during your journey:

- **Wash your hands** regularly, especially before eating.

- **Avoid touching your face**, particularly your eyes, nose, and mouth, as this can introduce germs.

- If you feel unwell, contact the ship's medical center immediately to prevent the spread of illness to others.

What to Do If You Feel Sick:

If you begin to feel unwell, it's important to rest and hydrate. For seasickness, follow the advice from the ship's medical staff, and don't hesitate to reach out for **medications** or **treatment** as needed.

Contact Information for Seasickness and Travel Illness:

- **Cruise Ship Health and Safety (e.g., Norwegian Cruise Line)**:

  o **Contact**: info@ncl.com | +1 305-436-4000.

  o **Website**: www.ncl.com

  o **Address**: Norwegian Cruise Line, 7665 Corporate Center Drive, Miami, FL 33126, USA.

Chapter 13

Travel Safety: Norwegian Laws and Customs

Norway is a beautiful and safe country to visit, but it's always helpful to be aware of local laws and customs to ensure a smooth and respectful trip. By understanding the rules and respecting cultural norms, you can enjoy your time in Norway while avoiding any misunderstandings or legal issues.

Norwegian Laws You Should Know

While Norway is known for its high level of safety and welcoming atmosphere, there are some key laws that visitors should keep in mind:

Drinking Age:

In Norway, the legal age for purchasing alcohol is **18 years old** for beverages with an alcohol content under 22%, and **20 years old** for beverages with higher alcohol content. Alcohol is sold only in **specialty stores** (called **Vinmonopolet**), and not in regular supermarkets. It's important to be mindful of the legal drinking age and always carry identification if you're planning to buy alcohol.

Drugs:

Norway has strict laws against **illegal drugs**. The possession, use, and trafficking of drugs are punishable by heavy fines or prison time. Always avoid any contact with illicit substances, as penalties are severe.

Public Behavior:

Norwegians value **respect for personal space** and **politeness**. Public drunkenness is frowned upon, and noisy behavior can be considered disruptive. It's best to be aware of your surroundings and maintain a respectful demeanor, especially in public spaces.

Smoking:

Norway is largely **smoke-free**, with smoking banned in **public indoor spaces** such as restaurants, public transport, and certain outdoor areas. Make sure to smoke only in designated areas, which are usually clearly marked.

Customs and Etiquette

While Norway is generally open and accepting, it's always good to follow local customs and etiquette:

Politeness:

Norwegians are known for their polite and reserved nature. It's customary to greet people with a firm handshake, but avoid being overly familiar. **Personal space** is important, so avoid standing too close to others in queues or public places.

Tipping:

Tipping is **not mandatory** in Norway, but it's appreciated for good service. In restaurants, it's common to leave a **5-10%** tip if the service is exceptional. However, if the service charge is included in the bill, there is no need to tip.

Punctuality:

Norwegians value **punctuality** and expect people to be on time for appointments, tours, and social gatherings. Arriving late is considered disrespectful.

Contact Information for Travel Safety:

- **Norwegian Police**:

    - **Contact**: postmottak@jd.dep.no | +47 22 24 52 03.

    - **Website**: www.politiet.no

    - **Address**: Politidirektoratet, Postboks 8005 Dep, 0030 Oslo, Norway.

    - **Opening Hours:** Monday–Friday: 8:00 AM – 4PM.

- **Vinmonopolet (Alcohol Stores)**:
    - **Contact**: info@vinmonopolet.no | +47 22 01 50 00.
    - **Website**: www.vinmonopolet.no
    - **Address**: Dronning Eufemias gate 11, 0150 Oslo, Norway.

Staying Safe While Exploring the Shore

Exploring the shorelines of Norway's stunning fjords offers plenty of opportunities for adventure and sightseeing. However, there are a few key safety tips to keep in mind while on land to ensure you have a safe and enjoyable experience.

General Safety Tips While on Shore

Wildlife Safety:

Norway's fjords are home to a variety of wildlife, including **seals**, **whales**, and **reindeer**. If you plan to explore the countryside, be aware of local animals and give them plenty of space. If you're going on **wildlife excursions**, always listen to your guide's instructions for maintaining a safe distance from animals.

Hiking Safety:

Norway's hiking trails are some of the most beautiful in the world, but they can also be dangerous, especially in the **mountainous** and **rocky** regions. Make sure to stick to marked trails and always check the weather before setting out, as conditions can change quickly. Wear appropriate footwear and bring plenty of water and snacks. If you plan to hike in remote areas, it's advisable to take a **guided tour** for added safety.

Weather Considerations:

The weather in Norway can change rapidly, especially in coastal and mountainous areas. Always bring a **weatherproof jacket**, **layers**, and **appropriate gear** to protect yourself from wind and rain. Never underestimate the weather even in summer, as conditions can be unpredictable. Keep an eye on weather reports to avoid getting caught in dangerous conditions.

Water Safety:

If you're taking part in water-based activities such as **kayaking**, **boating**, or **swimming**, always wear a **life jacket** and make sure to follow local safety instructions. The fjords can have strong currents, and water temperatures can be very cold, even in summer. If you're not an experienced swimmer, consider joining a **guided boat tour** for safety.

Safety in Norwegian Cities

Norwegian cities, including **Oslo**, **Bergen**, and **Tromsø**, are generally very safe for tourists. However, like any destination, it's important to be cautious of petty theft, especially in busy tourist areas. Always keep an eye on your personal belongings and avoid displaying large amounts of cash or valuables.

Emergency Contacts:

In case of emergencies, **Norwegian police** and **ambulance services** are available through the national emergency number, **112**. If you're lost or need help, don't hesitate to ask locals for assistance—Norwegians are generally friendly and helpful.

Contact Information for Safety While Exploring the Shore:

Norwegian Tourist Safety Information:

- **Contact:** info@visitnorway.com | +47 23 28 29 00.
- **Website:** www.visitnorway.com
- **Address:** Grev Wedels plass 9, 0151 Oslo, Norway.
- **Opening Hours:** Monday–Friday: 08:00AM – 4:00PM.

Norwegian Red Cross (Emergency Services):

- **Contact**: post@redcross.no | +47 22 05 40 00.
- **Website:** www.rodekors.no
- **Address**: Hausmannsgate 7, 0186 Oslo, Norway.
- **Opening Hours:** Monday–Friday: 08:00AM–4PM.

This chapter provides essential **travel safety** tips, focusing on **Norwegian laws**, **customs**, and **exploring the shore** safely. With practical advice on everything from **wildlife safety** to **hiking precautions,** you'll be well-prepared to enjoy your fjord adventure with peace of mind.

Chapter 14

Responsible Tourism: Preserving the Fjords

The Norwegian Fjords are one of the world's most stunning natural wonders, and preserving their beauty is essential for future generations. Responsible tourism plays a key role in protecting these pristine environments. As travelers, we have a duty to minimize our impact on the fjords while still enjoying all the incredible experiences they offer.

What Is Responsible Tourism?

Responsible tourism is about making ethical decisions that ensure your travels do not harm the environment, culture, or economy of the places you visit. It's about respecting the local communities, following sustainable practices, and leaving the destination better than you found it. In the case of the fjords, this means protecting the delicate ecosystems and minimizing pollution.

Leave No Trace:

One of the simplest ways to practice responsible tourism is by following the **Leave No Trace** principle. This means picking up after yourself, disposing of waste properly, and avoiding littering. Stick to marked trails when hiking to prevent damage to the environment, and avoid disturbing wildlife during your excursions.

Eco-Friendly Travel Choices:

When planning your visit, consider making eco-friendly choices such as opting for **electric vehicles** or **sustainable modes of transport**. Many cruise ships now offer **eco-friendly** options with **low emissions** or **hybrid engines**, which help reduce the environmental impact on the delicate fjord ecosystems.

Sustainable Cruise Options:

There are several cruise lines that operate with a strong commitment to **sustainability**. These ships minimize their environmental footprint through advanced **wastewater treatment systems**, **energy-efficient technologies**, and **eco-friendly shore excursions** that help preserve the fjords' natural beauty.

Supporting Local Communities

Another important aspect of responsible tourism is supporting local businesses that prioritize **sustainability** and **cultural preservation**. Choose to buy products that are locally made and environmentally friendly. When staying in fjord towns, look for

eco-certified accommodations or restaurants that source ingredients locally and practice sustainable farming methods.

Contact Information for Responsible Tourism:

Norwegian Sustainable Tourism:

- **Contact:** info@visitnorway.com | +47 23 28 29 00.
- **Website:** www.visitnorway.com
- **Address:** Grev Wedels plass 9, 0151 Oslo, Norway
- **Opening Hours:** Monday–Friday: 08:00AM – 4:00PM.

Green Key Certification (Sustainable Tourism):

- **Contact**: greenkey@fee.no | +47 22 00 25 00.

- **Website**: www.greenkey.fee.no

- **Address:** Bislett Stadion, 0368 Oslo, Norway.

- **Opening Hours:** Monday–Friday: 9:00 AM–4PM.

- **Price Range:** Application Fee: NOK 7,500; Annual Levy: NOK 12,000 + NOK 70 per room; Audit Fee: NOK 6,000 + travel costs.

Wildlife Protection and Eco-Friendly Activities

The Norwegian Fjords are home to diverse wildlife, including seals, whales, and a variety of seabirds. Protecting these animals and their habitats is critical, and eco-friendly activities are an excellent way for travelers to connect with nature while minimizing their impact.

Wildlife Conservation Efforts

Norway has strict laws to protect its wildlife and natural habitats. The government works closely with conservation organizations to preserve the ecosystems of the fjords, ensuring that wildlife such as **whales**, **seals**, and **fish species** are not endangered by human activities.

Whale Watching and Responsible Tours:

While whale watching is a popular activity in Norway, it's essential to ensure that you are booking a tour with an operator that follows **ethical guidelines** for wildlife viewing. Responsible whale-watching tours focus on **minimizing disturbance** to marine life and educate participants about the importance of preserving these majestic creatures.

Seal and Bird Watching:

The fjords are home to a variety of other wildlife, such as **seals** and **sea eagles**. Tours that focus on **eco-friendly wildlife observation** help protect the animals by maintaining a respectful distance and limiting the time spent in sensitive areas.

Sustainable Fishing Practices:

Fishing in the fjords is a part of local tradition, but it must be done in a way that does not harm the ecosystem. **Sustainable fishing practices** are essential to maintaining the delicate balance of marine life in the fjords. When buying fish or seafood during your visit, choose products that have been certified by **sustainable fisheries**.

Eco-Friendly Activities to Enjoy in the Fjords

There are numerous ways to explore the fjords while supporting conservation efforts. Choose eco-friendly activities such as:

Kayaking:
Paddle through the fjords in a **silent kayak**. This non-intrusive way to explore allows you to get up close to the natural surroundings and wildlife without disturbing the environment.

Electric Boat Tours:

Opt for **electric boats** or hybrid boats instead of traditional gas-powered vessels. These eco-friendly tours reduce pollution and provide a quieter, more peaceful way to explore the fjords.

Eco-Friendly Hiking:

Hiking is an excellent way to experience the beauty of the fjords. When hiking, remember to stay on designated trails to avoid damaging delicate plant life. Always bring biodegradable products and minimize waste.

Cycling Tours:

Cycling is another sustainable way to explore Norway's stunning landscapes. Many towns and regions offer **guided cycling tours** through the fjords, allowing you to enjoy the scenery while reducing your environmental impact.

Contact Information for Wildlife Protection and Eco-Friendly Activities:

Norwegian Nature and Wildlife Protection (Norwegian Society for the Conservation of Nature):

- **Contact**: naturvern@naturvernforbundet.no | +47 23 10 96 10.
- **Website**: www.naturvernforbundet.no

- **Address**: Mariboes gate 8, 0183 Oslo, Norway.
- **Opening Hours:** Monday–Friday: 9:00 AM–4PM.

Norwegian Environment Agency

- **Contact**: postmottak@kld.dep.no | +47 22 24 57 11.
- **Website**: www.environmentagency.no
- **Address**: P.B.8013 Dep, 0030 Oslo, Norway.
- **Opening Hours:** Monday–Friday: 8:00 AM–4PM.

Eco-Friendly Boat Tours (e.g., Adventure Tours):

- **Contact**: post@adventuretours.no | +47 95 76 63 85.
- **Website**: https://www.adventuretours.no/
- **Address**: Adventure Tours AS, 6876 Skjolden, Norway.
- **Opening Hours:** Monday to Sunday.

This chapter provides detailed insights into **responsible tourism** and **eco-friendly activities** in the Norwegian Fjords. By choosing sustainable travel options and supporting wildlife protection efforts, you can help preserve these breathtaking landscapes and ecosystems for future generations.

254 | Norwegian Fjords Cruise Travel Guide 2025

Chapter 15

The Environmental Impact of the Cruise Industry & Sustainable Travel in Norway

This chapter delves into the environmental impact of the cruise industry, focusing on issues like air and water pollution, waste management, and the cruise industry's efforts toward sustainability. It highlights how traditional cruise ships contribute to pollution and waste, while also outlining the steps being taken to reduce these effects, such as the use of **greener technologies** and **sustainable shore excursions**. As a traveler, you're encouraged to support **eco-conscious cruise lines** and reduce your own environmental footprint.

Additionally, this chapter provides practical advice on traveling sustainably in Norway. It emphasizes eco-friendly transportation options like **electric vehicles**, **public transport**, and **cycling**. The chapter also encourages supporting **local, sustainable businesses**, engaging in **eco-friendly activities** such as hiking and kayaking, and being mindful of waste. These practices help ensure that your visit to the Norwegian fjords not only preserves its natural beauty but also benefits local communities.

The Cruise Industry's Impact on the Environment

Cruising through the Norwegian Fjords is an unforgettable experience, but it's important to acknowledge the environmental impact that the cruise industry can have. While many cruise lines are making strides in sustainability, the sheer scale of the industry still poses challenges to the fragile ecosystems in which it operates.

Air and Water Pollution

One of the primary environmental concerns related to the cruise industry is the emission of **greenhouse gases**. Many traditional cruise ships run on **fossil fuels**, contributing to air pollution and climate change. Additionally, cruise ships are known to discharge wastewater, sewage, and chemicals into the ocean, which can damage marine ecosystems, including the pristine waters of the fjords.

Waste Management

Cruise ships generate a significant amount of waste, from plastic to food scraps, which is often not disposed of in an environmentally responsible manner. While many cruise lines have made improvements in waste management systems, including recycling and composting programs, the overall environmental footprint remains large.

What's Being Done:

In recent years, the cruise industry has been making efforts to reduce its environmental impact. Many cruise lines are transitioning to **greener technologies**, such as **liquefied natural gas (LNG)** engines, which emit fewer pollutants. Some ships are now equipped with **advanced wastewater treatment plants** to prevent pollution from entering the oceans.

Sustainable Shore Excursions:

Many cruise lines now offer **sustainable shore excursions** that minimize environmental impact. These excursions focus on eco-friendly activities like **hiking**, **electric boat tours**, and **bicycle tours**, which help reduce the carbon footprint of shore-based activities.

What You Can Do:

As a passenger, you can also make a difference by supporting cruise lines that prioritize sustainability. Look for cruise lines that are certified by **green initiatives** or have made commitments to reduce emissions and waste. Choose ships that use **alternative fuels** and those that focus on **carbon offset programs**. Additionally, be mindful of your own waste and environmental impact during your trip.

Contact Information for Cruise Industry and Environmental Impact:

- **Cruise Industry Environmental Standards (e.g., Cruise Lines International Association)**:
  - **Contact**: info@cruising.org | +1 202-759-9370.
  - **Website**: www.cruising.org
  - **Address**: 1201 F Street NW, Suite 250, Washington, DC 20004, USA.

How to Travel Sustainably in Norway

Traveling sustainably is not only important for preserving the natural beauty of Norway but also for ensuring that local communities benefit from tourism in a responsible and equitable way. Here are some tips on how to minimize your environmental impact while enjoying all that Norway has to offer.

1. Opt for Sustainable Transportation

Norway offers a variety of **eco-friendly transportation** options that help reduce your carbon footprint:

Electric Vehicles (EVs):

Norway has one of the highest rates of **electric vehicle** ownership in the world. Many car rental companies offer **electric cars** for eco-conscious travelers. When renting a car, look for an **EV rental** to reduce emissions while exploring the country.

Public Transport:

Norway has an extensive and efficient **public transportation system**, including trains, buses, and ferries. **Trains** are particularly eco-friendly, and many routes offer spectacular views of the fjords, making them a great alternative to driving.

Cycling:

Norway is a fantastic place to explore by bike. Many cities offer **bike-sharing programs**, and there are numerous **cycling routes** around the fjords that allow you to immerse yourself in nature without contributing to pollution.

2. Support Local and Sustainable Businesses

When visiting Norwegian towns and villages, support local businesses that focus on sustainability. This includes **restaurants** that use **locally sourced ingredients** from responsible farmers, and **artisan shops** selling **handmade, eco-friendly crafts**. Local products are not only unique and high quality, but they also support the local economy and reduce the carbon footprint associated with mass-produced goods.

3. Engage in Eco-Friendly Activities

Norway offers plenty of activities that allow you to enjoy the outdoors without negatively impacting the environment. Some of these include:

Hiking:

Hiking is one of the eco-friendliest ways to explore Norway's stunning landscapes. Stick to **marked trails** to minimize your impact on the surrounding nature.

Wildlife Watching:

Take part in **responsible wildlife tours** that emphasize minimal disruption to animals and their habitats. **Eco-friendly whale watching**, for example, allows you to observe these magnificent creatures without causing harm.

Kayaking:

Paddling through the fjords in a **kayak** or **canoe** is a peaceful and sustainable way to experience the area while respecting nature. Many tour companies now offer **electric-powered boats** for eco-friendly cruises.

4. Be Mindful of Your Waste

Whether you're on the ship or on land, it's important to minimize waste. Bring your own **reusable water bottle**, **shopping bags**, and **utensils** to avoid single-use plastics. Many Norwegian towns offer **recycling stations** where you can properly dispose of waste.

This provides detailed guidance on how you can travel sustainably in Norway, covering everything from **eco-friendly transportation** to **supporting local businesses**. With your thoughtful approach to travel, you can help protect the incredible Norwegian environment and support local communities.

Chapter 16

Maximizing Your Cruise Experience: Money-Saving Tips, and Staying Connected

This chapter provides practical advice on making the most of your Norwegian Fjords cruise experience, from **money-saving tips** to **staying connected**. It covers **budget-friendly strategies**, such as booking early, traveling off-peak, and exploring DIY shore excursions. The chapter also offers **photography tips** for capturing the fjords' stunning landscapes, including the best times for photos, equipment recommendations, and how to photograph wildlife responsibly.

For those ashore, it suggests how to **maximize shore time**, including planning ahead, using public transport, and engaging in local experiences. Finally, it addresses how to **stay connected** while cruising, with tips on **Wi-Fi access** onboard, **phone roaming** in Norway, and **local SIM cards** for better coverage. Whether you're looking to save money, capture the perfect shot, or keep in touch, this chapter ensures a smooth, enjoyable, and eco-conscious voyage.

Money-Saving Tips: Deals and Offers

Cruising the Norwegian Fjords is an incredible experience, but it doesn't have to break the bank. There are plenty of ways to save money on your trip while still making the most of the adventure. Whether you're looking for discounts on your cruise booking or affordable activities once you're in Norway, here are some money-saving tips to help you enjoy a budget-friendly cruise experience.

Book Early for Better Rates

One of the best ways to save money on your Norwegian Fjords cruise is by **booking early**. Cruise lines often offer substantial discounts for bookings made well in advance, and you'll have more cabin options to choose from. Early bookings also allow you to snag **better deals** on **shore excursions**, as these can sell out quickly during peak season.

Look for Special Offers and Discounts

Many cruise lines offer **special deals** during certain times of the year. These might include discounted rates for early bookings, last-minute deals, or special offers for seniors, families, or loyalty members. Keep an eye out for **promotions** and **flash sales**, especially during the off-peak seasons.

Travel Off-Peak

The high summer months of **June to August** are the busiest (and most expensive) time to visit the Norwegian Fjords. However, you can still experience stunning views and pleasant weather by traveling during the shoulder seasons—**May** and **September**. These months tend to offer lower prices on both cruises and excursions while avoiding the large crowds.

Consider the All-Inclusive Packages

If you like the idea of not having to worry about paying for each meal, drink, or excursion separately, consider booking an **all-inclusive cruise package**. Many cruise lines offer packages that include meals, drinks, gratuities, and some shore excursions, which can help save money in the long run.

DIY Shore Excursions

While booking shore excursions through the cruise line is convenient, it can often be more expensive. Instead, consider exploring on your own. **Public transportation** in Norway is efficient and affordable, and many of the fjord towns have free or inexpensive activities, such as hiking, sightseeing, or visiting local museums.

Getting the Best Photos of the Fjords

The Norwegian Fjords are one of the most photogenic places on Earth, with their towering cliffs, serene waters, and vibrant landscapes. If you want to capture the beauty of the fjords, here are some tips to help you take the best possible photos during your trip.

Best Time for Photos

The **golden hour**—the period shortly after sunrise and before sunset—provides the soft, warm light that enhances the beauty of the fjords. This is the perfect time to take landscape shots of the fjords, as the light illuminates the cliffs and water in a stunning way.

- **Summer**: During the summer months, the long days provide plenty of time for outdoor photography. The Midnight Sun offers unique opportunities to capture breathtaking photos of the fjords bathed in natural light at any hour.

- **Winter**: If you're visiting in winter, the low light and snow-capped mountains provide a dramatic backdrop for photography. The contrast between the dark waters and the snow-covered landscape can create striking images.

Framing the Shot

The best photos of the fjords often include some foreground element to give a sense of scale. Look for **boats**, **trees**, or even **hikers** to add depth to your shots. Framing with a **leading line**, such as a path, road, or river, can also make your photos more visually compelling.

Camera Tips

- **Wide-Angle Lens**: A wide-angle lens is ideal for capturing the vast landscapes of the fjords. It allows you to capture more of the breathtaking scenery in a single frame.

- **Tripod**: If you're shooting in low light conditions or want to capture the water's movement, a **tripod** is essential for stable shots.

- **Drone Photography**: For stunning aerial views of the fjords, consider using a **drone**. Just make sure to check the local regulations before flying it.

Capturing Wildlife

When photographing wildlife, always respect their space and avoid getting too close. Use a **telephoto lens** to capture animals like whales, seals, and birds from a distance, ensuring you don't disturb them while still getting great shots.

Contact Information for Scenic Tours:

- **Norwegian Scenic Routes:**

  o **Contact**: info@nationaltouristroutes.no | +47 22 07 30 00.

  o **Website**: www.nasjonaleturistveger.no

  o **Address**: Norwegian Public Roads Administration, Postboks 8142 Dep., 0033 Oslo, Norway.

How to Make the Most of Your Shore Time

One of the highlights of a Norwegian Fjords cruise is the time spent exploring the towns, villages, and landscapes onshore. Whether you're in **Bergen**, **Tromsø**, or **Geiranger**, each port offers unique experiences. Making the most of your shore time ensures you get the most out of your journey, and with a little planning, you can enjoy your time on land while avoiding stress or rushing.

1. Plan Ahead and Prioritize

Shore excursions often sell out quickly, so it's a good idea to **book your tours in advance** to secure your spot. However, if you prefer exploring independently, research the top sights and activities available in the port before you arrive. Make a list of what interests you most, and decide how much time you can realistically spend at each location.

Research the Port:

For example, if you're stopping in **Tromsø**, you might want to prioritize seeing the **Northern Lights** or visiting the **Polaria Arctic Center**. If you're stopping in **Bergen**, don't miss the **Bryggen Wharf**, a UNESCO World Heritage site, and the **Fløibanen Funicular** for panoramic views of the city.

2. Explore on Foot or By Public Transport

The fjord towns are often small, and many of the main attractions are within walking distance from the port. Take a stroll through **old town** areas, visit local markets, or find a **café** with scenic views. For farther destinations, **public transport** in Norway is reliable and affordable, with **buses** and **trains** providing easy access to surrounding areas.

Walking Tours:

Many ports offer **guided walking tours**, which are an excellent way to learn about the area's history and culture while seeing the key sights.

3. Don't Forget to Factor in Downtime

While it's tempting to fill every moment with activities, it's also important to have some downtime. Use some of your shore time to relax and enjoy the local atmosphere. **Find a quiet spot** by the water or a local park and take in the scenery at your own pace. This will help you avoid feeling rushed and give you a chance to recharge before heading back to the ship.

4. Consider Local Experiences

In addition to the usual sightseeing, try to engage with the local culture through **hands-on experiences**. Whether it's tasting local delicacies, joining a **Sami cultural workshop**, or going on a **seafood tasting tour**, these activities offer a deeper connection to the places you visit.

Sustainable Options:

If you want to travel more sustainably, look for **eco-friendly shore excursions** that minimize environmental impact while offering an immersive experience. Many local guides also focus on **preserving the environment** and educating travelers on responsible tourism practices.

5. Be Mindful of Time

It's important to be mindful of the time, especially when traveling back to the ship. Always keep track of the **all-aboard time** and aim to return at least **15-30 minutes** before it. Ports can be busy, and it's easy to lose track of time while exploring, so plan accordingly.

Contact Information for Shore Excursions and Activities:

- **Tromsø Tourism**:
  - **Contact**: info@visittromso.no | +47 77 61 00 00.
  - **Website**: www.visittromso.no

- Address: Storgata 83, Postbox 311, 9253 Tromsø, Norway.

- Opening Hours: Monday–Friday: 09:00AM–5:00PM | Saturday: 09:00AM–4:00PM | Sunday: 10:00AM–3:00PM.

- **Bergen Tourist Information**:

  - Contact: info@visitBergen.com | +47 55 55 20 20.

  - Website: www.visitBergen.com

  - Address: Strandkaien 3, 5013 Bergen, Norway.

  - Opening Hours: Monday–Sunday: 9:00 AM – 4PM.

Staying Connected: Wi-Fi, Phone, and Roaming Information

While cruising through the Norwegian Fjords offers a chance to disconnect and enjoy the stunning scenery, staying connected to friends, family, or work may be important for some. Here's everything you need to know about staying connected while on board and exploring onshore.

1. Wi-Fi Onboard the Ship

Most cruise ships offer **Wi-Fi**, but the speed and cost can vary. Some ships have **free Wi-Fi** in certain public areas, but this is often limited or slow. For more reliable internet access, you can purchase Wi-Fi packages, which are typically available in **different tiers** (pay-as-you-go or unlimited packages).

What to Expect:

- Expect to pay for **internet access**. Prices can vary depending on the cruise line, but Wi-Fi on ships is often more expensive than what you're used to at home. It's often priced by the minute or by the amount of data used.

Tips for Saving on Wi-Fi:

- **Connect in port**: When you're in port, try to find a **local café** or restaurant that offers **free Wi-Fi** to avoid onboard charges. Many towns and cities in Norway offer free **public Wi-Fi** in areas like **town squares** or **museums**.
- **Offline Options**: Consider downloading maps, entertainment, or important information before your trip to minimize your need for internet access during the cruise.

2. Phone Roaming in Norway

Before you leave, it's essential to check with your **mobile provider** about **roaming charges** for Norway. International roaming fees can be high, so it's wise to know the cost of calling, texting, and using data while you're in Norway.

International Roaming:

- Most major phone networks have **international roaming** agreements with Norwegian carriers, but the rates can vary widely. You may want to look into **international plans** or **data packs** that offer better rates for Norway.

Local SIM Cards:

- For longer stays or if you need more reliable data, consider buying a **local SIM card** in Norway. Many Norwegian mobile providers offer affordable SIM cards with data plans for short-term visitors, which can be a cost-effective alternative to international roaming.

3. Staying Connected While on Shore

When you're off the ship and exploring Norway, staying connected is easier than ever, thanks to the country's reliable **mobile network**. Norway has excellent **cell coverage**, even in remote areas, so you should have no problem staying connected. Public Wi-Fi is also available in most major cities and towns, though the connection can vary depending on location.

Using Apps:

- Many travelers rely on mobile apps for navigation, restaurant recommendations, and booking local activities. Popular apps like **Google Maps** and **TripAdvisor** are very useful when you're exploring Norwegian cities.

4. Emergency Contacts

In case of an emergency, having a local contact number is essential. Norway's emergency number is **112** for police, **113** for medical emergencies, and **110** for fire services.

Contact Information for Roaming and Connectivity:

- **Telenor (Norwegian Mobile Provider)**:

  o **Contact**: support@telenor.no | +47 678 90 000.

  o **Website**: www.telenor.no

  o **Address:** Snarøyveien 30, N-1360 Fornebu, Norway.

  o **Opening Hours:** Monday–Friday: 9:00 AM – 5:00 PM.

This chapter offers essential tips for making the most of your **shore time** while **saving money** and **staying connected** during your Norwegian Fjords cruise. Whether you're making the most of your time on land or staying in touch with loved ones, these tips will ensure a smoother and more enjoyable experience.

Chapter 17

Sample Itineraries for Every Traveler: A Comprehensive Guide to Exploring the Norwegian Fjords

---

This chapter offers a range of sample itineraries tailored to various types of travelers, ensuring that everyone can make the most of their time in the stunning Norwegian Fjords. For those with limited time, the one-day itinerary offers an immersive experience in Bergen, featuring iconic sights like **Bryggen Wharf, Mount Fløyen**, and a scenic fjord cruise. The three-day itinerary expands to explore **Geiranger, Ålesund**, and other key locations, providing a balance of history, nature, and adventure. For a more leisurely experience, the seven-day itinerary takes travelers through **Bergen, Sognefjord, Geirangerfjord**, and **Tromsø**, offering a complete immersion into Norway's beauty. Nature lovers can enjoy a three-day outdoor adventure in Geirangerfjord and the Lofoten Islands, while romantic couples can experience intimate moments in Bergen and Ålesund.

Finally, families will appreciate a fun-filled three-day itinerary that includes kid-friendly activities, such as visiting aquariums, fjord cruises, and hiking trails.

One-Day Itinerary: A Complete Norwegian Fjords Experience

For travelers with just one day to explore the Norwegian Fjords, this itinerary brings you the perfect mix of nature's beauty, history, and culture, ensuring you experience the highlights of this stunning region.

- **Morning:** Start your day in **Bergen**, Norway's gateway to the fjords. Begin with a visit to the **Bryggen Wharf** (Bryggen, 5003 Bergen), a UNESCO World Heritage site filled with colorful wooden houses and cobbled streets. Here, you can wander through small boutiques, coffee shops, and galleries. Afterward, take the **Fløibanen Funicular** to the top of **Mount Fløyen** (Fløibanen, 5014 Bergen) for panoramic views of the city and surrounding fjords.

- **Midday:** Head to the **Fish Market** (Torget, 5014 Bergen), where you can sample fresh Norwegian seafood, from king crab to smoked salmon. Grab a traditional **reker (shrimp)** sandwich or try some **raspeballer**, a local dumpling dish. After lunch, embark on a fjord cruise along the **Sognefjord**. This scenic journey takes you through the fjord's breathtaking landscapes, with steep cliffs, cascading waterfalls, and peaceful waters.

- **Afternoon:** Embark on a **fjord cruise** from Bergen's harbor to **Nærøyfjord**, one of Norway's most stunning fjords. As you glide along the calm waters, enjoy breathtaking views of steep cliffs, waterfalls, and pristine landscapes. The boat trip is the perfect way to experience the grandeur of the fjords in a short amount of time.

- **Evening:** End your day with dinner at **Bryggen Tracteursted** (Bryggen 2, 5003 Bergen), a restaurant known for serving traditional Norwegian dishes with a modern twist. Enjoy a cozy meal while gazing out over the fjord, then take a leisurely walk along the **Harbor Promenade** to soak in the serene evening atmosphere.

Three-Day Itinerary: Exploring the Wonders of Norway's Fjords

With three days to explore the stunning beauty of the Norwegian Fjords, this itinerary offers a mix of cultural discovery, outdoor adventure, and spectacular natural scenery.

- **Day One: Bergen and Fjord Views;** Start your journey in **Bergen**, exploring the **Bryggen Wharf**, **Fløibanen Funicular**, and **Fish Market** as detailed in the **One-Day Itinerary**. After lunch, take the **Flåm Railway** to **Flåm** (near Sognefjord), one of the world's most scenic train journeys. Once in Flåm, visit the **Aurland Lookout** for sweeping views of the fjord and the surrounding mountains. Enjoy a leisurely dinner in a fjordside restaurant, known for its freshly caught fish and local delicacies.

- **Day Two: Geiranger and the Majestic Geirangerfjord;** On your second day, head to **Geiranger** (Geiranger, 6216), one of the most beautiful fjord towns in Norway. Enjoy a scenic cruise along **Geirangerfjord**, a UNESCO World Heritage site, where you will be surrounded by majestic mountains and waterfalls such as the **Seven Sisters**. Afterward, take a hike to **Dalsnibba** (Dalsnibba, 6216 Geiranger), one of the highest points in the area, for panoramic views of the fjord and its surroundings.

- **Day Three: Ålesund and Coastal Beauty**; On your final day, head to the charming coastal town of **Ålesund** (Ålesund, 6003), known for its Art Nouveau architecture. Spend the morning exploring the town's beautiful buildings and walking along the promenade. In the afternoon, enjoy a relaxing fjord cruise along the **Hjørundfjord**, where you can take in the stunning scenery of towering peaks, secluded villages, and crystal-clear waters.

Seven-Day Norwegian Fjords Itinerary: A Complete Week of Adventure and Culture

A week in the Norwegian Fjords allows you to explore the region at a leisurely pace, immersing yourself in its stunning natural landscapes and rich cultural heritage.

Day One: Bergen – Gateway to the Fjords; Start your journey in Bergen, Norway's second-largest city, with a visit to **Bryggen** and the **Fløibanen Funicular** for stunning city views. In the afternoon, set sail for a fjord cruise to **Sognefjord**, Norway's longest fjord. Make a stop at **Flåm** and take the **Flåm Railway** for a scenic ride through the mountains.

Day Two: Exploring Sognefjord and its Villages; Spend the day cruising along **Sognefjord**, visiting quaint fjord-side villages like **Gudvangen** and **Balestrand**. Stop for a leisurely lunch in **Balestrand**, where you can enjoy the panoramic views over the fjord before continuing your journey.

Day Three: Geirangerfjord and the Seven Sisters; Cruise into **Geirangerfjord** and marvel at its incredible waterfalls, such as the **Seven Sisters** and **The Suitor**. In the afternoon, take a hike to **Dalsnibba**, one of the highest viewpoints in the area, for a spectacular view over the fjord.

Day Four: Ålesund – The Art Nouveau Town; Explore **Ålesund**, known for its stunning Art Nouveau architecture. Spend the day discovering the town's unique buildings, coastal views, and beautiful streets. In the afternoon, embark on a boat trip to **Hjørundfjord**, famous for its dramatic peaks and secluded villages.

Day Five: Tromsø – The Gateway to the Arctic; Arrive in **Tromsø** (Tromsø, 9008), located far above the Arctic Circle. Visit the **Arctic Cathedral** and **Polaria**, a unique Arctic aquarium, before spending the afternoon exploring the city's museums and cultural sights. End your day with a cable car ride to **Mount Storsteinen** for exciting views.

Day Six: Lofoten Islands – A Natural Paradise; Spend the day in the **Lofoten Islands** (Lofoten, 8370), a region known for its rugged landscapes, white sandy beaches, and beautiful fishing villages. Explore the charming village of **Reine**, hike the scenic trails, and visit the **Lofoten Viking Museum** for a glimpse into Norway's Viking past.

Day Seven: Return to Bergen; On your final day, sail back to **Bergen**, taking in the last views of the Norwegian coastline. Spend your final hours in Bergen exploring the **Fish Market** and enjoying a farewell meal of freshly caught seafood.

Three-Day Outdoor Adventure and Nature Lovers' Itinerary in the Norwegian Fjords

This itinerary is designed for those seeking outdoor adventure and a connection with nature in the stunning fjord landscapes.

- **Day One: Geirangerfjord and the Seven Sisters;** Start your adventure with a cruise along **Geirangerfjord**. Enjoy the spectacular view of **Seven Sisters** Waterfall and **The Suitor**. Afterward, hike up to **Dalsnibba** for panoramic views of the fjord. The area is known for its rugged beauty, perfect for nature lovers.

- **Day Two: Pulpit Rock and Lysefjord**; Take a morning hike to **Pulpit Rock** (Preikestolen), one of Norway's most iconic hiking spots. From the top, you'll have stunning views of **Lysefjord** below. Afterward, spend the afternoon relaxing and taking in the beauty of the fjord, with options for kayaking or a relaxing boat tour.

- **Day Three: Lofoten Islands Adventures** Explore the dramatic **Lofoten Islands**, where you can kayak in the fjords, go hiking to remote beaches, or enjoy a boat trip to see the **Northern Lights**. Spend your evening in the quaint village of **Reine**, soaking in the natural beauty of the region.

Three-Day Romantic Getaway in the Norwegian Fjords

For couples seeking a romantic escape in the Norwegian Fjords, this three-day itinerary offers intimate moments, scenic beauty, and relaxation.

- **Day One: Bergen – A Beautiful Start to Your Journey:** Start your romantic getaway in **Bergen**, exploring the picturesque **Bryggen** and enjoying a cable car ride to **Mount Fløyen**. In the evening, enjoy a candlelit dinner at a cozy harbor-side restaurant, offering local delicacies and stunning views of the city.
- **Day Two: Geirangerfjord and Waterfalls;** Cruise through **Geirangerfjord**, enjoying views of the **Seven Sisters Waterfall**. In the afternoon, visit **Dalsnibba** for stunning mountain vistas and relax with a quiet dinner in **Geiranger**.
- **Day Three: Ålesund – Coastal Charm**; Explore **Ålesund**, with its romantic streets and stunning architecture. Take a walk along the **Ålesund coastline** and enjoy a private sunset cruise, soaking in the breathtaking views. Finish your trip with a farewell dinner at a waterfront restaurant.

Three-Day Family Fun Itinerary in the Norwegian Fjords

Designed for families, this itinerary offers a mix of fun and adventure for all ages in the Norwegian Fjords.

- **Day One: Bergen and Fløibanen Funicular** Start your adventure in **Bergen** with a visit to **Bryggen** and a ride up **Mount Fløyen** on the **Fløibanen Funicular**. Once at the top, enjoy the panoramic views and let the kids explore the playground and trails. Afterward, visit the **Bergen Aquarium** for an exciting educational experience.
- **Day Two: Geirangerfjord Adventure** Take a **fjord cruise** in **Geirangerfjord**, visit the **Seven Sisters Waterfall**, and enjoy a family-friendly hike. Afterward, head to **Geiranger** for dinner at a local family-friendly restaurant.
- **Day Three: Ålesund and the Coastal Adventure**; Head to **Ålesund** and explore the town's unique architecture. Spend the afternoon at the **Atlanterhavsparken Aquarium**, where kids can learn about marine life, then finish the day with a family-friendly boat tour of the **Hjørundfjord**, a perfect way to wrap up your adventure.

Chapter 18

Essential Apps, Resources, and Contacts for Your Norwegian Fjords Adventure

---

Planning your Norwegian Fjords adventure can be overwhelming, but with the right tools at your fingertips, the experience becomes seamless and enjoyable. This chapter provides an in-depth look at the essential apps, resources, and official contacts that will help you navigate your journey. Whether you're hiking remote trails, cruising through stunning fjords, or discovering hidden cultural gems, these tools will ensure you're always prepared. From top travel apps like **Norgeskart** for detailed maps, to **Visit Norway's app** for personalized recommendations, each resource is designed to enhance your experience.

We also cover key websites for booking cruises and shore excursions, and introduce you to local tour operators who can provide unforgettable adventures in the fjords. Additionally, you'll find important tourist information centers and embassy contacts, ensuring you have access to help whenever you need it. With these invaluable resources, your trip to the Norwegian Fjords will be as smooth as the waters you'll cruise on.

Essential Travel Apps for the Norwegian Fjords

Traveling through the Norwegian Fjords can involve a lot of adventure, and having the right apps at your fingertips can simplify navigating through cities, fjords, and even remote areas. From weather updates to hiking trail guides, here's a list of the must-have apps for your Norwegian Fjords adventure.

Norgeskart (Norwegian Map App)

This app is perfect for those looking to explore the fjords' rugged landscapes, as it provides detailed maps of Norway, including hiking trails, road routes, and points of interest.

- **Website:** www.norgeskart.no
- **Features:** Topographic maps, offline access, route planning for hiking and driving.
- **Tip:** Ideal for exploring remote areas like the Lofoten Islands and hard-to-reach fjords such as **Hjørundfjord**.

Visit Norway App

This official app by Innovation Norway is an all-in-one resource for discovering Norway's highlights, including the fjords. It provides detailed information on attractions, activities, events, and essential travel tips.

- **Website:** www.visitnorway.com
- **Features:** Interactive maps, events calendar, activity recommendations, and offline access.
- **Tip:** Use the app to discover hidden gems and local recommendations that are not always included in mainstream tourist guides.

Yr.no (Norwegian Weather App)

Weather can change quickly in the Norwegian Fjords, especially in areas near the coast or higher altitudes. The **Yr.no** app, developed by the Norwegian Meteorological Institute, provides detailed and up-to-date weather forecasts, which is crucial when you're planning outdoor activities.

- **Website:** www.yr.no
- **Features:** Hourly weather updates, multi-day forecasts, alerts for severe weather conditions.
- **Tip:** Always check the weather before embarking on fjord cruises or mountain hikes, particularly in regions like **Geirangerfjord** or **Trollheimen**.

Ruter (Public Transport App)

The **Ruter** app is essential for public transport within Norway, particularly if you're traveling to and around the larger cities like **Oslo**, **Bergen**, or **Trondheim**, and need to access bus, tram, and metro routes.

- **Website:** www.ruter.no
- **Tip:** Use this app for smooth public transport connections when traveling between towns like **Bergen** and **Voss**.

Google Maps

While not fjord-specific, **Google Maps** is indispensable when exploring Norway's winding coastal roads or urban centers. Whether you're heading to a remote village or navigating a mountain road, Google Maps offers reliable navigation to make your trip smooth.

- **Website:** www.google.com/maps
- **Features:** Turn-by-turn navigation, offline maps, real-time traffic updates.
- **Tip**: Download offline maps for areas with limited connectivity, such as parts of **Pulpit Rock** or **Rondane National Park**.

Fjord Tours App

For those seeking to book scenic fjord cruises, **Fjord Tours** provides a seamless experience for booking boat trips and multi-day tours along the Norwegian fjords, such as the **Sognefjord** or **Hardangerfjord**.

- **Website:** www.fjordtours.com
- **Features:** Booking options, tour descriptions, itineraries for multi-day fjord trips.
- **Tip:** Book your tours in advance during the high season (summer months), as the most popular fjord routes tend to fill up quickly.

Komoot

Outdoor enthusiasts will find **Komoot** an invaluable app for planning hikes and cycling routes throughout the Norwegian Fjords. The app offers detailed trail maps, elevation profiles, and offline navigation, perfect for those hiking the famous **Romsdalseggen Ridge** or **Kjerag**.

- **Website**: www.komoot.com
- **Features**: Offline maps, hiking and cycling route recommendations, elevation data.
- **Tip**: Plan your hiking route in advance and download the map for offline use, especially in remote mountain areas.

Fjord Norge App

For those eager to experience everything the Norwegian Fjords have to offer, **Fjord Norge** is a must-have app. This app provides detailed information about fjord cruises, scenic drives, hiking trails, and accommodation options across the fjord region.

- **Website**: www.fjordnorway.com
- **Features**: Travel routes, information on fjord tours, and curated recommendations.
- **Tip**: Check out the **"Scenic Routes"** section to discover hidden gems around the fjords, perfect for both first-timers and repeat visitors.

TripAdvisor

For detailed reviews on everything from attractions and restaurants to hotels and guided tours, **TripAdvisor** is an indispensable app. It's perfect for finding the best-rated experiences in the Norwegian Fjords, whether you're looking for local food spots or unique fjord cruises.

- **Website**: www.tripadvisor.com
- **Tip**: Use the app to find hidden gems recommended by other travelers, such as **Lofoten Islands** or **Trolltunga**, which may not always be listed in mainstream guides.

Official Tourist Information and Visitor Contacts for the Norwegian Fjords

Having access to reliable tourist information can significantly enhance your visit to the Norwegian Fjords. Whether you need assistance with planning your route, finding local experiences, or handling emergencies, Norway's official tourist centers offer valuable resources.

Visit Norway Tourism Board

The official tourist board for Norway provides an abundance of resources for visitors, from comprehensive travel guides to local tourism offices across the country. They are also the go-to source for information on sustainability and eco-friendly travel options in the fjords.

- **Website:** www.visitnorway.com
- **Contact:** +47 23 28 29 00.

Bergen Tourist Information Center

For travelers arriving in **Bergen**, this is the main hub for tourist information. The center offers free maps, brochures, and expert advice on how to explore Bergen and the nearby fjords.

- **Website:** www.visitBergen.com

- **Contact**: +47 55 55 20 20.
- **Address**: Strandkaien 3, 5013 Bergen, Norway.
- **Opening Hours:** Monday–Sunday: 9:00 AM – 4PM.
- **Tip:** Ask about current events, such as local festivals or seasonal markets in **Bryggen** or along the **Fish Market**.

Ålesund Tourist Information Center

Ålesund, known for its Art Nouveau architecture, is a popular stop for travelers exploring the fjords. This center provides information on local attractions, as well as recommendations for boat tours and outdoor activities.

- **Website**: www.visitalesund.com
- **Contact**: +47 70 15 76 00.
- **Address**: Skateflukaia, 6002 Ålesund, Norway.
- **Opening Hours:** Monday–Friday: 08:30AM–4:00PM; Saturday–Sunday: Closed.
- **Tip:** Don't forget to ask about boat tours to nearby islands like **Giske** and **Godøy** or local hikes like the **Aksla Viewpoint**.

Flåm Tourist Information Center

Situated at the heart of **Flåm**, a popular base for exploring **Aurlandsfjord**, this tourist center offers a variety of resources to enhance your fjord experience, from information on **Flåmsbana** to local food experiences.

- **Website**: www.norwaysbest.com
- **Contact**: +47 57 63 14 00.
- **Address**: Stasjonsvegen, 5742 Flåm, Norway.
- **Opening Hours:** Monday–Sunday: 08:00 AM–6:45 PM.
- **Tip:** The Flåm Railway is one of the most iconic experiences in Norway. Ask about discounts for combined fjord cruises and train rides.

Regional Visitor Centers

Apart from the major cities, there are also smaller visitor centers spread throughout the fjords, providing localized information on attractions, local history, and hiking trails. Here are a few notable ones:

- **Sogndal Tourist Office** (Sogndalsdalen, 6856 Sogndal, Norway).

- **Geiranger Tourist Office** (Stranda, 6216 Geiranger, Norway).

- **Lofoten Islands Tourist Office** (Torget 18, 8300 Svolvær, Norway).

Embassy Contacts

While Norway is one of the safest countries in the world, it's always a good idea to have embassy contact details handy, especially in case of lost passports, legal matters, or emergencies.

U.S. Embassy in Oslo

For American travelers, the U.S. Embassy in Oslo is the place to go for consular services, such as emergency passport replacement or legal help.

- **Website:** no.usembassy.gov
- **Contact**: +47 21 30 85 40.
- **Address**: Morgedalsveien 36, 0378 Oslo, Norway.
- **Opening Hours:** Monday–Friday: 8:00AM – 3:30PM; Saturday–Sunday: Closed.
- **Tip:** Register for the **Smart Traveler Enrollment Program (STEP)** to receive important travel updates.

British Embassy in Oslo

The British Embassy in Oslo provides consular services to British nationals in Norway, including emergency assistance, passport renewals, and general advice.

- **Website:** www.gov.uk/world/organisations/british-embassy-oslo
- **Contact:** +47 23 13 27 00.
- **Address:** Thomas Heftyes gate 8, 0244 Oslo, Norway.
- **Opening Hours:** 24 hours, daily.
- **Tip:** It's advisable to call ahead and schedule an appointment if you require urgent consular services.

Canadian Embassy

The Canadian Embassy in Oslo provides consular services, including assistance with visas, passports, and other services for Canadian citizens living or traveling in Norway.

- **Website:** https://www.international.gc.ca/
- **Contact:** +47 22 99 53 00.
- **Address:** Wergelandsveien 7 (4th floor), 0244 Oslo, Norway.
- **Opening Hours:** Monday–Friday: 08:30 AM–12:30 PM (by appointment); 1:00 PM–4:30 PM (by appointment).
- **Tip:** Canadians can also enroll in the **Registration of Canadians Abroad** for real-time alerts and updates.

Local Guides and Operators for your Norwegian Fjords Cruise Travel

Hiring a local guide or operator can greatly enhance your experience, whether you're hiking in remote regions, cruising through the fjords, or taking part in unique activities like whale watching or fjord fishing. Here are some of the Norwegian Fjords top-rated operators to consider:

Fjord Tours

Fjord Tours is a reputable operator offering a wide range of fjord tours and experiences, from day trips to multi-day cruises. They provide packages that combine scenic cruises, bus trips, and iconic rail journeys like the **Flåm Railway**.

- **Website:** www.fjordtours.com
- **Features**: Guided tours, scenic train rides, fjord cruises, and multi-day packages.
- **Tip:** Book in advance during the summer months when tours are in high demand.

Green Gold of Norway

Green Gold of Norway provides eco-friendly tours in and around the fjords, with a focus on sustainability and education.

They offer tours that cover both the natural beauty and cultural heritage of the region.

- **Website:** www.greengoldofnorway.com
- **Tip:** Ask about their **eco-friendly cruises** that minimize your carbon footprint while exploring the fjords.

Go Fjords

Go Fjords is another operator specializing in eco-friendly tours and activities, including fjord cruises, hiking, and bike tours. They emphasize sustainability in all their offerings.

- **Website**: www.gofjords.com
- **Features**: Guided tours, kayaking, hiking, and fjord cruises.
- **Tip**: Inquire about their eco-friendly tours, especially the **electric-powered boats** used for some of their fjord cruises.

Geiranger Fjord Service

For an intimate experience of **Geirangerfjord**, **Geiranger Fjord Service** offers private boat tours, hiking trips, and eco-friendly excursions that highlight the fjord's incredible landscapes.

- **Website:** www.geirangerfjord.no
- **Features:** Boat tours, hiking, and eco-tourism activities.

- **Tip:** Combine a boat tour with a hike to **Dalsnibba** for breathtaking views of the fjord.

Arctic Adventures AS

For those seeking a more rugged adventure, **Arctic Adventures AS** specializes in arctic exploration, offering dog-sledding, glacier tours, and wilderness hikes in areas like **Tromsø** and **Svalbard**.

- **Website:** https://arcticadventuretours.no/
- **Features:** Glacier hikes, dog-sledding, and wildlife tours.
- **Tip:** Book early for winter tours to catch the Northern Lights.

Norway in a Nutshell®

This iconic tour operator offers a one-day package that includes travel by boat, train, and bus to some of Norway's most famous fjords, including **Nærøyfjord** and **Flåm**.

- **Website**: www.norwaynutshell.com
- **Features**: Guided tours of Norway's fjords, transportation through multiple scenic routes.
- **Tip**: Book in advance during the high season, as these tours are extremely popular.

Useful Websites for Cruise Bookings and Planning

Planning a cruise through the stunning Norwegian Fjords offers an unforgettable experience, and having the right resources at your fingertips can make the process easier and more enjoyable. From booking the cruise itself to finding exciting shore excursions and understanding the best times to visit, these websites offer valuable insights and tools to help you plan your perfect journey.

Cruise Line Websites

Booking directly through the cruise line's official website is one of the most straightforward ways to secure your Norwegian Fjords cruise. These websites offer detailed itineraries, flexible options, and exclusive promotions. By browsing the official sites, you can often access the best deals and understand the nuances of each cruise line's offerings.

Viking Ocean Cruises

Viking Ocean Cruises is renowned for its upscale experience, offering luxurious ships and carefully curated itineraries that showcase the stunning landscapes and culture of the Norwegian

Fjords. Their focus is on cultural immersion, scenic vistas, and fine dining, making it an ideal choice for travelers seeking a sophisticated and enriching journey.

- **Website**: www.vikingcruises.com

Norwegian Cruise Line

Norwegian Cruise Line (NCL) is famous for its relaxed, flexible cruising style. Known for dynamic onboard entertainment and a variety of dining options, NCL's itineraries are perfect for travelers looking for a balance between adventure and leisure. They offer numerous itineraries in the Norwegian Fjords, providing various options for every type of cruiser.

- **Website**: www.ncl.com

Hurtigruten

For travelers looking to truly immerse themselves in the wilderness of the Norwegian coast, Hurtigruten is a specialist in expedition cruises. Their ships are designed for smaller, more intimate voyages, allowing guests to access remote fjords, the Arctic, and even the Lofoten Islands. Hurtigruten's itineraries emphasize exploration, local culture, and wildlife, offering the ultimate adventure.

- **Website**: www.hurtigruten.com

Cruise Planning Websites

These platforms are great tools to help you compare different cruise lines, search for special deals, and gain advice from seasoned cruisers. From reviewing the latest offers to providing insight into shore excursions, these websites can guide your decision-making process and ensure you get the most out of your cruise.

Cruise Critic

Cruise Critic is one of the most comprehensive cruise planning websites, offering user reviews, cruise line comparisons, and suggestions for shore excursions. Whether you're looking to compare itineraries or find tips from experienced travelers, Cruise Critic has a wealth of information to help you plan every detail of your Norwegian Fjords adventure.

- **Website**: www.cruisecritic.com

CruiseDirect

CruiseDirect provides an easy-to-use platform for comparing prices across various cruise lines. This site enables you to access competitive rates for Norwegian Fjords cruises and offers a convenient way to view itineraries, special deals, and discounts.

It's perfect for cruisers who want to ensure they're getting the best possible deal on their trip.

- **Website**: www.cruisedirect.com

By using these reliable websites, you'll be able to book your Norwegian Fjords cruise, plan shore excursions, and access all the information you need to ensure a smooth and unforgettable trip. Whether you're seeking adventure, relaxation, or cultural discovery, these resources will help you craft the perfect Norwegian Fjords journey.

Conclusion

As we arrive at the final pages of this guide, it's time to pause, reflect, and truly appreciate the journey you've either just taken—or are about to begin—through the breathtaking Norwegian Fjords. This isn't just a cruise; it's a deeply moving experience, where the power of nature meets centuries of history, and where every bend in the fjord unveils a new story waiting to be felt more than simply told.

From the serene reflections on the **Sognefjord** to the dramatic cliffs of **Geiranger**, every bend in the water feels like it's revealing a secret meant just for you. The cry of a sea eagle overhead, the thunder of a waterfall in the distance, the soft mist of a morning fjord cruise—these are not just moments to photograph but to feel with your whole being. Norway's fjords don't just impress; they invite you to be present, to breathe deeper, and to see the world through a wider, more thoughtful lens.

Traveling through the fjords isn't about rushing from port to port—it's about leaning into the slower rhythm of life here. It's about letting yourself be changed by nature's scale and serenity. Whether you hiked to the edge of **Pulpit Rock** and felt your breath catch at the sight of **Lysefjord** stretching far below, or simply sipped hot coffee on a cold morning while watching snow-capped peaks drift by, those moments matter. They are the kind of memories that don't just fade into vacation photos, but stay with you like an old friend.

While this guide has done its best to prepare you with all the practical tools, tips, and insider knowledge to navigate your journey, the most meaningful part of your trip will be what happens when you put the map down and let Norway reveal itself to you. Maybe it will be the hushed quiet of a **Lofoten beach**, or the laughter of new friends made during a shore excursion. And so, as you prepare to disembark and carry your stories home, know this: you've touched a piece of Norway that many will only ever imagine. You've sailed through ancient glacial carvings, felt the brisk sting of **Arctic air**, and stood at the edge of cliffs that have watched centuries unfold. The fjords have a way of staying with you—long after the ship has docked, long after the suitcase is unpacked. They'll linger in your thoughts when the world feels too loud, too fast, or too unfamiliar.

Norway has a way of staying with you long after the cruise ends. It lives in your senses—the taste of fresh salmon straight from the grill, the chill of glacial air on your cheeks, the way twilight lingers just a little longer in the north. It teaches you something vital: that nature, when untouched and respected, gives back something far greater than we could ever expect.

Thank you for letting this guide be part of your journey. It has been an honor to help you navigate one of the most spectacular corners of the world. May your travels continue to bring you awe, peace, and wonder. And whenever your heart calls you back to the deep blue fjords, the sharp peaks, and the endless sky of Norway—know that the fjords will be waiting, unchanged, timeless, and always ready to welcome you home.

Safe travels, and until we meet again—ha det bra.

TRAVEL PLANNER

TRAVEL PLANNER BONUS

TRAVEL PLANNER

DATE:
DURATION:
DESTINATION:

PLACES TO SEE:
1.
2.
3.
4.
5.
6.
7.

LOCAL FOOD TO TRY:
1.
2.
3.
4.
5.
6.
7.

DAY 1	DAY 2	DAY 3

DAY 4	DAY 5	DAY 6

NOTES

EXPENSES IN TOTAL:

TRAVEL

DATE:
DURATION:

DESTINATION:

PLACES TO SEE:
1.
2.
3.
4.
5.
6.
7.

LOCAL FOOD TO TRY:
1.
2.
3.
4.
5.
6.
7.

DAY 1	DAY 2	DAY 3

DAY 4	DAY 5	DAY 6

NOTES

EXPENSES IN TOTAL:

PLANNER

TRAVEL PLANNER

DATE:
DURATION:

DESTINATION:

PLACES TO SEE:
1.
2.
3.
4.
5.
6.
7.

LOCAL FOOD TO TRY:
1.
2.
3.
4.
5.
6.
7.

DAY 1

DAY 2

DAY 3

DAY 4

DAY 5

DAY 6

NOTES

EXPENSES IN TOTAL:

TRAVEL

DATE:
DURATION:

DESTINATION:

PLACES TO SEE:
1.
2.
3.
4.
5.
6.
7.

LOCAL FOOD TO TRY:
1.
2.
3.
4.
5.
6.
7.

DAY 1	DAY 2	DAY 3

DAY 4	DAY 5	DAY 6

NOTES

EXPENSES IN TOTAL:

PLANNER

TRAVEL PLANNER

DATE:
DURATION:
DESTINATION:

PLACES TO SEE:
1.
2.
3.
4.
5.
6.
7.

LOCAL FOOD TO TRY:
1.
2.
3.
4.
5.
6.
7.

DAY 1

DAY 2

DAY 3

DAY 4

DAY 5

DAY 6

NOTES

EXPENSES IN TOTAL:

Printed in Dunstable, United Kingdom